Journey into Classic Crinkles and Sugar Sparkles

Classic Crinkles and Sugar Sparkles: Timeless Favorites

Olivia Stewart

Table of Contents

INTRODUCTION

Welcome to the enchanting world of sweet indulgence and timeless delights in "Journey into Classic Crinkles and Sugar Sparkles: Classic Crinkles and Sugar Sparkles: Timeless Favorites." This e-book invites you on a delectable adventure, exploring the rich history, artistry, and heartwarming traditions behind classic crinkles and sugar sparkles—two iconic categories of cookies that have stood the test of time.

In the opening chapter, we embark on a delightful journey into the realm of cookies, where every bite carries the essence of nostalgia and the warmth of cherished memories. These classic crinkles and sugar sparkles are more than confections; they embody tradition, creativity, and the joy of sharing something homemade with those we hold dear.

As we delve into the following pages, we uncover these timeless favorites' fascinating history. From their humble beginnings to becoming beloved treats worldwide, these cookies have been woven into cultural celebrations and everyday moments. Discover the stories behind the recipes, the people who shaped them, and the cultural significance that makes each bite a trip down memory lane.

The journey doesn't stop at history; it extends into the heart of baking itself. Chapter by chapter, we explore the art of crafting these delectable treasures. Learn about essential tools, perfecting the techniques, and overcoming common challenges. Whether you're a seasoned baker or just starting your culinary adventure, this e-book is your guide to creating perfect crinkles and sparkles every time.

This is not just a collection of recipes; it's an invitation to create, innovate, and savor the joy of baking. Join us as we celebrate the magic of classic crinkles and sugar sparkles —a celebration of tradition, creativity, and the timeless pleasure of sharing delicious moments with those we love. Welcome to a journey that transcends generations and leaves a trail of sweetness in its wake.

CHAPTER I

History of Classic Crinkles and Sugar Sparkles

Origins and evolution of classic cookie recipes

The origins and evolution of classic cookie recipes trace a fascinating journey through time, blending cultural influences, culinary innovations, and the simple pleasure of satisfying a sweet tooth. Cookies, those delightful morsels of baked goodness, have a history as diverse as the flavors they encompass.

Cookies have a long culinary history dating back to ancient Persia, when they were first made as little cakes. Early cookies were not the bite-sized treats we know today but nourishing and easily portable sustenance for travelers and explorers. These early versions, akin to what we now call "biscuits," often comprised an essential mix of flour, water, and sweeteners. Over time, the concept of cookies spread across the globe, adapting to each region's available ingredients and culinary traditions.

The evolution of classic cookie recipes gained momentum during the Middle Ages in Europe. As trade routes expanded, ingredients like sugar, spices, and exotic fruits became more accessible, transforming simple cookies into delectable confections. The first documented examples of modern-style cookies featuring butter and sugar emerged in 17th-century Europe. Dutch and British immigrants brought these recipes to America, laying the foundation for today's diverse cookie landscape.

The 18th and 19th centuries they marked a pivotal period in the evolution of classic cookies. With the Industrial

Revolution, baking became more accessible to the general populace as ingredients became mass-produced. This era saw the rise of iconic cookies like the gingerbread man, oatmeal cookies, and sugar cookies, each rooted in regional traditions and family recipes.

The chocolate chip cookie, arguably the quintessential classic, existed in the 1930s. Ruth Wakefield, the owner of the Toll House Inn in Massachusetts, is credited with accidentally creating this masterpiece when she added chunks of a Nestle chocolate bar to her cookie dough, expecting them to melt and make chocolate cookies. Instead, the chocolate retained its form, and the chocolate chip cookie was born. This serendipitous discovery led to the popularity of chocolate chip cookies and catapulted Nestle's chocolate sales.

In the mid-20th century, they witnessed the rise of convenience and packaged foods, influencing the evolution of classic cookie recipes. Pre-packaged cookie mixes and ready-to-bake dough made it easier for home bakers to whip up a batch of cookies without the labor-intensive process of measuring and mixing individual ingredients. While these innovations provided convenience, they also sparked a resurgence of interest in traditional, homemade cookies as people sought to recapture the authentic flavors of bygone eras.

The late 20th century and early 21st century brought about a renaissance in cookie creativity. Bakers began experimenting with flavors, textures, and ingredients, giving rise to many variations on classic recipes. From artisanal bakeries to home kitchens, the cookie landscape became a canvas for culinary expression, incorporating diverse ingredients like sea salt, exotic spices, and unconventional mix-ins.

Simultaneously, dietary preferences and restrictions spurred the evolution of classic cookie recipes to accommodate a wider audience. Gluten-free, vegan, and allergen-friendly versions of traditional cookies emerged, allowing individuals with dietary restrictions to indulge in the timeless joy of cookies.

In recent years, the internet and social media have played a significant role in the evolution of classic cookie recipes. Online platforms have become virtual recipe exchanges, allowing bakers worldwide to share their innovations, adaptations, and personal twists on timeless favorites. This global exchange of ideas has led to the fusion of traditional recipes with diverse culinary influences, resulting in unique and boundary-pushing cookie creations.

In conclusion, the origins and evolution of classic cookie recipes are a testament to the adaptability and creativity of the culinary world. From humble beginnings as practical, portable sustenance to the intricate and diverse flavors we enjoy today, cookies have evolved alongside cultural shifts, technological advancements, and changing tastes. The rich history of classic cookies is a chronicle of culinary innovation and a reflection of the human experience—a journey of exploration, creativity, and enduring joy in a simple, sweet indulgence.

Cultural significance and traditions

The cultural significance and traditions surrounding food are profound reflections of a society's history, values, and identity. Within this rich tapestry of culinary heritage, the role of nutrition extends beyond mere sustenance; it becomes a powerful symbol of shared identity, familial bonds, and cultural continuity. One of the most evocative expressions of this connection is found in the diverse and often deeply rooted traditions associated with the preparation and consumption of food. This section explores the cultural significance and traditions surrounding food, delving into how culinary practices shape and are shaped by the societies they emerge from.

Food has always held a central place in the rituals and traditions of cultures worldwide. From communal feasts that mark religious celebrations to intimate gatherings centered around family recipes, sharing a meal transcends the boundaries of sustenance to become a collective experience. In many cultures, traditional dishes are imbued with layers of meaning, often carrying stories of migration, survival, and adaptation. Recipes are passed down through generations, each reflecting the cultural context of its time while preserving a connection to the past. These culinary traditions serve as a bridge between ages, fostering a sense of continuity and shared heritage.

In countries like Italy, where food is a cornerstone of cultural identity, traditional recipes are treated with reverence beyond mere gastronomy. The preparation of a dish like pasta sauce, for instance, is a ritualistic process handed down through families, with each iteration carrying the unique touch of the cook. Making and sharing these dishes becomes a form of cultural preservation, a way of maintaining a connection to one's roots, even in the face of societal change. The communal nature of food preparation and consumption fosters a sense of belonging and shared identity, reinforcing cultural bonds within families and communities.

Beyond the familial sphere, food plays a pivotal role in religious and ceremonial traditions. In India, for example, preparing sweets like laddoos and sharing food during festivals are culinary events and sacred rituals that reinforce spiritual connections. The ingredients, cooking methods, and presentation are often symbolic, aligning eating with spiritual and cultural values. Food becomes a tangible expression of religious devotion and cultural adherence, linking individuals to a broader tapestry of tradition and faith.

Furthermore, food's cultural significance extends to how it shapes social interactions and community dynamics.

Festivals and gatherings are often marked by specific culinary offerings, from the symbolic bread in religious ceremonies to the elaborate spreads during holidays. These shared meals catalyze social bonding, fostering community and belonging. Whether it's a potluck dinner, a barbecue, or a traditional tea ceremony, sharing food becomes a unifying force, breaking down barriers and creating spaces for dialogue and connection.

Culinary traditions also reflect the geographical and ecological contexts in which they emerge. In coastal regions, seafood often takes center stage, showcasing a community's reliance on the sea's bounty. In arid climates, where resourcefulness is paramount, traditional dishes may feature drought-resistant crops and preserved foods. Adapting recipes to local ingredients reflects the ingenuity of a community and underscores the interplay between the natural environment and cultural practices.

However, the globalization of food has brought both opportunities and challenges to culinary traditions. On one hand, the exchange of culinary ideas and ingredients has enriched the diversity of global cuisines. People can now savor flavors from different corners of the world, and cross-cultural fusion has given rise to innovative and exciting culinary creations. On the other hand, the homogenization of food due to mass production and global supply chains poses a risk to preserving authentic culinary traditions. As fast-food chains proliferate and convenience becomes a priority, there is a concern that the unique flavors and practices that define regional cuisines may need to be improved or recovered.

There has been a growing movement to celebrate and preserve culinary traditions in response to these challenges. Food festivals, culinary heritage initiatives, and the resurgence of interest in traditional cooking methods are testament to a collective effort to safeguard the cultural significance of food. Organizations and individuals are working to document, revitalize, and promote traditional recipes, ensuring they remain vibrant expressions of cultural identity in the face of modernization.

In conclusion, the cultural significance and traditions of food are integral to the human experience. Culinary practices are woven into the fabric of societies, reflecting diverse communities' stories, values, and shared histories. From the intimate setting of family kitchens to the grandeur of religious ceremonies, preparing and sharing food transcends its utilitarian purpose to become a powerful expression of cultural identity and continuity. As societies evolve, preserving and celebrating culinary traditions stand as a testament to maintaining a connection to our roots, fostering a sense of belonging, and honoring the rich tapestry of human heritage.

Iconic moments in cookie history

In the vast and delectable realm of culinary history, cookies occupy a special place, delighting taste buds and creating memorable moments for centuries. Iconic occasions that have influenced not just the baking industry but also the cultural and societal landscapes have defined the evolution of cookies. This section explores pivotal moments, from ancient origins to modern innovations, that have defined cookie history and contributed to the enduring love for these sweet treats.

The journey into cookie history begins in ancient Persia, where the concept of cookies first took shape. Originating as small cakes, these early precursors to cookies served a practical purpose as portable, easily preserved sustenance for travelers and explorers. The Persian empire's influence on the culinary world laid the groundwork for the evolution of baked goods, setting the stage for what would later become a global phenomenon.

Fast-forward to medieval Europe, where the Crusaders from the Middle East brought back exotic spices, including cinnamon, cloves, and nutmeg. The infusion of these aromatic ingredients into cookie recipes not only added depth of flavor but also signaled the beginning of a more sophisticated approach to baking. Cookies transitioned from basic sustenance to coveted indulgence enjoyed by the privileged few.

The Renaissance period witnessed the refinement of cookie recipes in Europe, with butter and sugar becoming prominent ingredients. These additions transformed cookies into more delicate and sweet confections, enjoyed by the aristocracy and making their way into the burgeoning middle class. As the art of baking advanced, cookies became an integral part of European culinary traditions, celebrated during festivities and special occasions.

In the 17th century, they brought Dutch and British immigrants to the shores of America, bringing their cherished cookie recipes. As the colonies developed, so did the American approach to cookies, incorporating local ingredients and adapting recipes to suit the available resources. Cookies became a symbol of hospitality and were often shared between neighbors and at community gatherings.

One of the most iconic moments in cookie history it occurred in the 1930s with the accidental creation of the chocolate chip cookie. Ruth Wakefield, the owner of the Toll House Inn in Massachusetts, intended to make chocolate cookies by adding pieces of Nestle chocolate to the dough, expecting the chocolate to melt and blend into the batter. To her surprise, the chocolate retained its shape, creating the first chocolate chip cookie. This serendipitous discovery not only revolutionized the world of cookies but also catapulted Nestle's chocolate sales and established the chocolate chip cookie as a quintessential American classic.

The mid-20th century saw the rise of convenience and packaged foods, influencing the evolution of cookies once again. Pre-packaged cookie mixes and ready-to-bake dough became staples in households across America, simplifying the baking process and making cookies more accessible to the general public. However, the popularity of these convenient options coexisted with a growing appreciation for traditional, homemade cookies.

The 1960s and 1970s marked a period of experimentation and innovation in cookie history. Home bakers began exploring creative variations, introducing unique flavors, textures, and mix-ins. From oatmeal raisin to peanut butter and beyond, the possibilities seemed endless. Cookie recipes were no longer confined to rigid traditions, allowing for a burst of creativity that paved the way for a diverse array of cookie options.

The 1980s and 1990s witnessed the emergence of gourmet cookies and specialty bakeries, elevating the humble cookie to a high-end indulgence. Artisanal bakers crafted cookies with premium ingredients, departing from mass-produced options. The demand for these elevated sweet treats reflected a cultural shift toward valuing quality and unique flavor combinations.

The turn of the century brought about a renewed interest in classic recipes, fueled by a desire to reconnect with nostalgic flavors and traditional baking techniques. Home bakers and professional chefs alike began revisiting time-honored recipes, putting a modern spin on classic cookies while preserving the essence of their heritage.

In recent years, the internet and social media have played a significant role in shaping cookie history. Online platforms have become virtual spaces for bakers to share their creations, exchange recipes, and showcase innovative techniques. The rise of food influencers and dedicated baking communities has contributed to the global sharing of cookie recipes, inspiring bakers worldwide to experiment with flavors, shapes, and decorations.

Furthermore, the demand for inclusive and diverse options has led to the development of cookies tailored to specific dietary preferences. Gluten-free, vegan, and allergen-friendly cookies have become increasingly popular, allowing individuals with dietary restrictions to enjoy the pleasure of cookies without compromise.

As we reflect on these iconic moments in cookie history, it becomes evident that cookies are more than just sweet treats; they are time capsules of cultural and culinary evolution. From their humble beginnings in ancient Persia to the chocolate-studded revelation in a Massachusetts kitchen, cookies have witnessed and adapted to the changing tides of history. They have evolved from practical sustenance to symbols of celebration, comfort, and creativity, leaving an indelible mark on our collective culinary consciousness.

In conclusion, cookies are a tale of innovation, adaptation, and the enduring joy derived from a simple yet extraordinary indulgence. Iconic moments in cookie history have shaped the evolution of baking and become woven into the fabric of cultural traditions and shared experiences. As we continue to celebrate and innovate within the world of cookies, we pay homage to the bakers, inventors, and culinary enthusiasts who have contributed to the delightful and delicious journey that is cookie history.

CHAPTER II

The Art of Baking

Essential baking tools and ingredients

In the realm of baking, where science meets artistry, the choice of tools and ingredients plays a pivotal role in the success of creating delightful confections. Essential baking tools and components form the backbone of the baking process, influencing everything from texture and flavor to the final presentation of the finished product. Aspiring bakers, seasoned pastry chefs, and home enthusiasts alike understand the importance of having a well-equipped kitchen and a carefully selected array of ingredients. This essay explores the significance of essential baking tools and elements, delving into the nuanced interplay between precision, creativity, and the alchemy that transforms critical components into delectable treats.

The essential utensils that facilitate the intricate dance of ingredients are at the heart of any baker's toolkit. Mixing bowls, measuring cups, and spoons are the unsung heroes, providing the foundation for accurate measurements and uniform blending. Whether the

mixing bowl is made of plastic, glass, or stainless steel, it

can affect the dough or batter's overall texture and temperature management. Measuring utensils, calibrated to precision, ensure that ingredients are added correctly, laying the groundwork for a successful bake.

Whether a humble hand mixer or a sophisticated stand mixer, the mixer is a workhorse in the baker's arsenal. Various attachments allow for efficient creaming, beating, and whipping, saving time and effort while achieving consistent results. The stand mixer, in particular, has become an iconic symbol of the modern kitchen, revolutionizing how batters are mixed and freeing up the baker's hands for other tasks.

Baking is a delicate science that requires precision, and accurate temperature control is paramount. The oven thermometer emerges as a crucial tool, ensuring that the oven's internal temperature matches the set dial, preventing under or over-baking. Pastry brushes, silicone spatulas, and offset spatulas are indispensable for applying glazes, smoothing batters, and achieving professional finishes. These tools are the extensions of a baker's hands, allowing for meticulous attention to detail.

Rolling pins, both traditional and French-style, are the artisans of dough manipulation. Their smooth, cylindrical surfaces help achieve the desired thickness and consistency in pie crusts, cookies, and pastries. Pastry cutters and dough scrapers assist in shaping and portioning, contributing to the overall precision of the baking process. The interplay between these tools is akin to a choreographed ballet, with each movement contributing to creating a culinary masterpiece.

In the realm of ingredients, flour stands as the cornerstone, providing structure and texture to a wide array of baked goods. The type of flour—whether all-purpose, bread flour, cake flour, or specialty flour like almond or coconut—determines the outcome. Flour also acts as a canvas for the baker's creativity, offering a blank slate that can be transformed into many delights.

Leavening agents, such as baking powder and baking soda, are the silent catalysts that bring rise and lightness to baked goods. Yeast, a living organism, is the magical ingredient responsible for the airy crumb and distinct flavor of bread. The careful balance of these leavening agents is a delicate dance that transforms dense mixtures into fluffy cakes, light pastries, and perfectly risen bread.

Sweeteners from granulated sugar to honey, maple syrup, and beyond contribute sweetness and caramelization to baked goods. The choice of sweetener influences not only the taste but also the texture and color of the final product. Brown sugar, with its molasses content, adds moisture and depth of flavor, while powdered sugar lends a velvety smoothness to icings and frostings.

Fats, like butter, oils, and shortening, are integral to achieving the desired tenderness and richness in baked goods. The temperature and type of fat used can significantly alter the texture of a dough or batter. With its distinctive flavor and ability to create flaky layers, butter is a fundamental component in many classic recipes.

With their emulsifying and binding properties, eggs contribute structure and moisture to baked goods. The number of eggs, as well as their size, influences the final texture and consistency. Egg whites, when whipped, can create peaks that result in airy meringues and light chiffon cakes, while egg yolks contribute richness and a golden hue.

Dairy products like milk, cream, and yogurt add moisture and flavor to baked goods. The choice between whole milk, buttermilk, or alternative dairy products affects the richness and acidity of the final product. Dairy also plays a crucial role in achieving the desired tenderness in pie crusts and the creamy texture in custards.

Flavorings, including extracts, spices, and zest, are the artists' palettes, infusing baked goods with distinctive aromas and tastes. Vanilla extract, the most ubiquitous flavoring, adds depth and warmth to various recipes. The careful balance of spices, from cinnamon and nutmeg to cardamom and ginger, elevates the sensory experience of cookies, cakes, and pastries.

The significance of essential baking tools and ingredients extends beyond their functional roles; they are the conduits through which creativity and tradition converge. Whether following a cherished family recipe or experimenting with innovative flavor combinations, bakers rely on these tools and ingredients to bring their visions to life. The tactile nature of baking, from measuring and mixing to kneading and shaping, fosters a connection between the baker and the craft.

In the pursuit of perfection, precision is paramount. Bakers meticulously measure and weigh each ingredient, aware that even the slightest deviation can alter the delicate balance of a recipe. The scientific nature of baking requires a systematic approach, where each step builds upon the last, culminating in a symphony of flavors, textures, and aromas. The use of essential tools, from accurate scales to reliable timers, ensures that the alchemy of baking unfolds seamlessly.

However, within this precision lies a paradox—the freedom to experiment and innovate. Baking, while rooted in science, is also an art form that encourages creativity and personal expression. Bakers may deviate from a traditional recipe, substituting ingredients, adjusting flavors, or incorporating unexpected elements to create something new. The transformative power of baking lies in the hands of those who understand the rules but aren't afraid to bend them.

The significance of essential baking tools and ingredients is most evident in the cultural and familial traditions they help preserve. Passed down from generation to generation, recipes become cherished heirlooms, encapsulating memories and stories within their measurements. The mixing bowl that witnessed a grandmother's hands, the rolling pin that shaped countless pie crusts—these tools become vessels of nostalgia, linking the present to a rich tapestry of shared history.

In many cultures, baking is intertwined with rites of passage, celebrations, and communal gatherings. Holiday traditions, whether it's making Christmas cookies, hot cross buns for Easter, or mooncakes for the Mid-Autumn Festival, are steeped in the symbolism of shared nourishment and joy. Baking becomes a language of love, a tangible expression of care and connection.

The cultural significance of essential baking tools and ingredients is also evident in the diverse global culinary traditions. From the intricate layers of French pastry to the bold flavors of Indian sweets, each culture brings its unique blend of tools and ingredients to the world of baking. Baking is a universal language that transcends borders, allowing people to connect through the shared experience of enjoying and creating baked delights.

As we navigate the intricate baking landscape, it becomes evident that essential tools and ingredients are not mere instruments but storytellers. They narrate tales of innovation, adaptation, and the timeless pursuit of perfection. The mixing bowl carries the echoes of countless recipes, the oven thermometer bears witness to temperature trials, and the spatula becomes a companion in folding and smoothing.

In conclusion, the significance of essential baking tools and ingredients is multifaceted, encompassing precision, creativity, tradition, and cultural richness. From the practical measuring cup to the aromatic vanilla extract, these elements form the alchemical blend that transforms raw ingredients into culinary masterpieces. As bakers embark on the timeless journey of kneading, folding, and baking, they become the custodians of a culinary heritage that extends beyond the confines of the kitchen, weaving a narrative that connects generations and cultures through the shared joy of delicious creations.

Tips for perfecting the art of cookie baking

In baking, mastering the art of crafting the perfect cookie is both a science and an art. From achieving the ideal balance of flavors to ensuring the right texture, cookie baking is a nuanced process that requires precision, patience, and a dash of creativity. This essay explores many tips to perfect the art of cookie baking, covering everything from ingredient selection to baking techniques and the transformative impact of attention to detail.

The foundation of exceptional cookies lies in the quality and proportion of ingredients. Selecting the suitable flour is crucial, as it determines the structure and texture of the cookie. All-purpose flour is a versatile choice for many recipes, but specific types, like bread or cake flour, can achieve the desired characteristics in certain cookies. Precision in measuring ingredients is paramount; investing in accurate measuring cups and spoons ensures that the delicate balance of flavors and textures is maintained.

The choice of sweeteners influences the sweetness level, moisture content, and color of the final product. Experimenting with different sugars, such as granulated, brown, or even alternative sweeteners, allows bakers to tailor their cookies to personal preferences. The interplay between sugars and fats, usually in butter, oil, or shortening, contributes to the cookie's tenderness, richness, and overall mouthfeel. Using high-quality fats can elevate the flavor profile of cookies, with butter imparting a distinctive richness and coconut oil adding a hint of tropical sweetness.

Eggs play a multifaceted role in cookie baking, contributing to structure, moisture, and flavor. The size and freshness of eggs matter; using eggs at room temperature ensures better incorporation into the batter. The careful balance between egg whites and yolks can be adjusted to achieve specific textures, with egg whites contributing to a lighter, fluffier result and egg yolks enhancing richness. Additionally, dairy products, such as milk or yogurt, can be incorporated for added moisture and flavor complexity.

Leavening agents, such as baking powder and baking soda, are essential for achieving the desired lift and texture of cookies. Baking powder is often used in recipes that require a softer, cakier texture, while baking soda, when activated by an acidic ingredient like brown sugar, contributes to a chewier result. Understanding the role of these leavening agents and their interaction with other ingredients empowers bakers to troubleshoot and adjust recipes as needed.

Flavorings are the palette with which bakers can unleash their creativity. Vanilla extract is ubiquitous and versatile, but experimenting with other extracts, such as almonds, citrus, or even unconventional choices like lavender or cardamom, can yield unique and delightful results. The careful addition of spices, such as cinnamon, nutmeg, or ginger, can elevate the flavor profile of cookies, adding depth and warmth. Zest from citrus fruits imparts brightness and complexity, while a touch of salt can balance sweetness and enhance overall flavor.

The incorporation of mix-ins, from chocolate chips and nuts to dried fruit or shredded coconut, allows for endless variations on classic recipes. The choice of mix-ins adds texture and flavor and provides an opportunity for personalization. Dark chocolate chunks may offer a rich, decadent experience, while white chocolate or butterscotch chips can bring sweetness and a hint of caramel. Nuts, when toasted before incorporation, contribute depth and crunch.

Mixing the cookie dough requires a delicate touch to achieve the desired texture. Overmixing can lead to tough cookies, as excess gluten development toughens the structure. The creaming method, where butter and sugar are beaten together until light and fluffy, is a common technique that introduces air into the dough, resulting in a tender crumb. Dry ingredients should be incorporated gradually to prevent overmixing, with flour added in portions and mixed just until combined.

Chilling the cookie dough before baking serves multiple purposes. It allows the fats to solidify, preventing excessive spreading during baking and contributing to a thicker, chewier texture. Chilled dough enhances the flavor profile as the ingredients meld and develop over time. Moreover, this step provides an opportunity to prepare the dough in advance, allowing for convenient and efficient baking later.

The technique of portioning and shaping cookie dough significantly influences the final appearance and texture of the cookies. Using a cookie scoop ensures uniformity in size, promoting even baking. For certain cookies, such as drop cookies or those with mix-ins, shaping the dough into balls by hand allows for a rustic, homemade appearance. Rolling the dough in sugar before baking creates a delightful exterior texture and adds a touch of sweetness.

The baking process requires attention to detail, from preheating the oven to the specified temperature. Oven thermometers provide an extra layer of accuracy, ensuring that the temperature inside the oven matches the setting on the dial. Proper spacing on the baking sheet is crucial to prevent cookies from merging during baking. Whether a light or dark aluminum or nonstick baking sheet is used, it can affect how quickly the cookies brown and how they look overall.

The duration of baking is a critical factor in achieving the desired texture. Cookies continue to set and firm up outside the oven, so slightly underbaking ensures a softer result. Timing may need adjustment based on individual oven characteristics, and periodic checking is recommended to prevent overbaking. The golden rule is to remove cookies from the oven when they appear slightly underdone and allow them to cool on the baking sheet for a few minutes before transferring to a cooling rack.

Cooling is the final step in the cookie-baking process and is as crucial as any other. Cookies continue to firm up as they cool, and this period allows flavors to meld and intensify. The choice of cooling rack, whether elevated or flat, can influence the airflow around the cookies and impact their texture. It is advisable to allow cookies to cool completely before storing, as warmth can lead to condensation and compromise texture.

Storing cookies properly preserves their freshness and flavor. Airtight containers or cookie tins prevent exposure to air and moisture, keeping the desired texture. Layering with parchment paper can prevent unwanted sogginess for cookies with different textures, such as crisp biscotti or delicate macarons. Cookies can also be frozen for extended storage, with careful packaging to prevent freezer burn.

The art of cookie baking extends beyond the technical aspects to encompass the joy of experimentation and personalization. Understanding the science behind ingredient interactions and baking techniques provides a solid foundation, but there is ample room for creativity and innovation. Bakers can explore unique combinations of flavors, experiment with textures, and even incorporate cultural influences to create signature cookies that reflect their style.

Moreover, sharing homemade cookies transcends the confines of the kitchen. Whether gifted to friends and family or shared at communal gatherings, cookies can evoke joy and create lasting memories. Perfecting the art of cookie baking is not merely about achieving a flawless result but also about savoring the journey, relishing the aroma that fills the kitchen, and creating moments of connection through the shared delight of a freshly baked cookie.

In conclusion, perfecting cookie baking is a blend of science, craftsmanship, and creativity. Each step in the process contributes to creating a delightful treat, from the selection of high-quality ingredients to the precision of measuring and mixing. Tips for achieving the perfect cookie extend from ingredient choices to baking techniques, offering a roadmap for bakers to navigate the nuanced world of cookie baking. Whether following a cherished family recipe or embarking on a culinary adventure of innovation, cookie baking is a timeless pursuit that brings joy, warmth, and a touch of sweetness to the heart of every baker and the homes they fill with the aroma of freshly baked cookies.

Common challenges and how to overcome them

The art of baking, while deeply rewarding, comes with its set of challenges that even the most seasoned bakers encounter. From the subtle nuances of ingredient interactions to the precise orchestration of baking techniques, common challenges in baking can be both frustrating and enlightening. This essay explores these challenges and offers insights into overcoming them, guiding bakers to navigate the complexities of the baking process with skill and confidence.

The careful balancing of ingredient amounts is a common baking challenge. Achieving the perfect harmony between flour, sugar, fats, leavening agents, and flavorings is essential for the success of any baked good. Too much flour can result in a dry and crumbly texture, while excess sugar may lead to overly sweet treats with undesirable browning. The challenge lies in understanding the role of each ingredient and adjusting ratios to achieve the desired taste and texture.

To overcome this challenge, precise measurement is paramount. Using accurate measuring cups and spoons ensures that each ingredient is added in the correct quantity. Additionally, investing in a kitchen scale allows for even greater accuracy, especially with ingredients like flour, where the weight can vary significantly based on humidity and packing density. Careful attention to ingredient proportions lays the foundation for successful baking.

Another common hurdle in baking is the need to achieve the perfect texture. Cookies may turn out too flat or puffy, cakes may be dense or overly crumbly, and bread may need more springiness. Texture challenges often stem from issues with leavening agents, overmixing the batter, or incorrect oven temperature. Understanding the science behind these factors is critical to overcoming texture-related challenges.

To address texture challenges, bakers can experiment with different leavening agents and their proportions. Baking powder and baking soda react differently in recipes, and adjusting their amounts can influence the rise and texture of the final product. Vigilance during mixing is crucial; overmixing can lead to excess gluten development, resulting in a tough texture. Finally, accurate oven temperature is imperative, and using an oven thermometer ensures that the stated temperature matches the actual conditions inside the oven.

The bane of many bakers' existence is the dreaded issue of overbaking or underbaking. It's a delicate dance to find the precise moment when cookies are golden but not browned, cakes are set but not dry, and bread has a perfectly golden crust. Overcoming this challenge requires vigilance, attention to detail, and understanding the specific visual and textural cues that indicate doneness.

One effective strategy is to rely on sensory indicators rather than strict adherence to baking times. The aroma of baked goods often changes as they approach doneness, and slight pressure on the surface can reveal the desired texture. Toothpick or skewer tests can also be employed to check for moist crumbs rather than raw batter. Awareness of these cues allows bakers to determine when their creations are confidently baked.

Achieving consistent results can be exceptionally irritating, especially when using different ovens or attempting to replicate a recipe across various batches. Inconsistencies may arise from variations in oven temperature, ingredient temperature, or even differences in mixing techniques. Overcoming this challenge requires meticulous attention to detail and a commitment to understanding the variables.

To address the consistency issue, bakers can invest in an oven thermometer to ensure accurate temperature readings. Bringing ingredients to room temperature before incorporating them into the recipe promotes even mixing and texture. Standardizing measuring techniques, such as spooning flour into measuring cups rather than scooping, can produce uniform results. Additionally, keeping a detailed record of each baking session, including variations and adjustments, allows continuous improvement and refinement.

The all-too-familiar challenge of a sinking cake or collapsed soufflé can be disheartening for any baker. Leavening agents play a crucial role in providing the desired lift, and their effectiveness can be compromised by factors such as outdated ingredients, improper storage, or incorrect usage. Understanding the role of leavening agents and addressing these potential pitfalls is critical to overcoming the deflation dilemma.

Using fresh and active leavening agents is crucial to keeping cakes from sinking. Baking powder and baking soda lose their potency over time, so regularly checking expiration dates and storing them in a cool, dry place is crucial. Correctly measuring leavening agents and incorporating them evenly into the batter are critical steps. Additionally, avoiding excessive oven door opening during baking helps maintain a consistent temperature and prevents abrupt changes that can lead to collapse.

Texture challenges can extend to pie crusts, with the common woe of a rigid or soggy crust plaguing many bakers. Achieving the elusive balance of a crisp exterior and tender interior requires a nuanced approach to handling the dough. Overworking the dough, using warm ingredients, or inadequate chilling can contribute to a tough crust, while failing to seal the crust properly may lead to sogginess.

To prevent a tough crust, the dough must be worked with care; too much kneading or rolling should be avoided. Using cold ingredients and allowing the dough to rest in the refrigerator before moving helps maintain a flaky texture. When faced with the challenge of a soggy crust, pre-baking the crust, known as blind baking, creates a barrier that prevents excess moisture from permeating the crust during the filling stage.

For many bakers, achieving the perfect balance of sweetness can be a problem. The challenge lies in distinguishing between satisfying a sweet tooth and avoiding an overpowering, cloying taste. The sweetness of baked goods is influenced not only by the quantity of sugar but also by the interaction with other ingredients. The type of sugar used, the inclusion of alternative sweeteners, and the interplay with flavors all contribute to the final perception of sweetness.

Bakers can experiment with different sugars and proportions to navigate the challenge of sweetness. Brown sugar, with its molasses content, adds depth and moisture to cookies and cakes. Exploring alternative sweeteners, such as honey, maple syrup, or agave nectar, can provide unique flavor profiles while reducing the overall sugar content. Additionally, adjusting the quantity of sugar based on personal preferences allows for a customized approach to sweetness.

The perennial problem of a cracked cheesecake surface is a common source of frustration for bakers aiming for a flawless presentation. The culprit is often the abrupt change in temperature during the cooling process, causing the cheesecake to contract and crack. Overcoming this challenge involves gradual cooling and minimizing drastic temperature fluctuations.

After the cheesecake has baked for the allotted amount of time, it is best to switch off the oven and let it cool down gently inside to avoid cracks. Crack prevention can also be achieved by preventing overmixing the batter and using a water bath during baking. The water bath provides a moist environment, preventing the surface of the cheesecake from drying out and cracking. During cooling, patience is critical to achieving a smooth and crack-free cheesecake.

The challenge of achieving the perfect rise in yeast-based breads is a hurdle many aspiring bakers face. Factors such as insufficient kneading, inadequate proofing time, or incorrect yeast activation can hinder the development of the desired airy structure. Understanding the nuances of yeast fermentation and the dough-rising process is essential to overcoming this challenge.

Ensuring the yeast is activated and alive is the first crucial step to promote a robust rise in yeast-based bread. Mixing the dough thoroughly, allowing for sufficient kneading, and providing adequate proofing time lets the yeast ferment and produce carbon dioxide, which creates the desired pockets of air in the bread. Warm water during the initial stages of breadmaking helps activate the yeast, contributing to a triumphant rise.

The challenge of achieving a consistent and vibrant color in baked goods, especially in the case of golden-brown crusts on bread or cookies, can be perplexing. Inconsistent oven temperatures, variations in ingredient quality, and the choice of sweeteners can impact the coloration of baked items. Addressing this challenge involves meticulous attention to oven conditions and ingredient selection.

Maintaining a steady oven temperature is crucial to ensure an even coloration in baked goods. Investing in an oven thermometer provides an accurate internal temperature gauge, allowing for adjustments as needed. Additionally, high-quality ingredients, such as fresh eggs and premium butter, contribute to a desirable color. Experimenting with different sweeteners and sugars can also impact browning, allowing bakers to achieve the perfect golden hue.

The challenge of achieving the perfect moisture balance in cakes, brownies, or quick breads can be a perplexing puzzle. An overly dry texture can result from overmixing the batter, using too much flour, or overbaking, while excessive moisture may stem from high water content in certain ingredients or underbaking. Navigating this challenge requires a keen understanding of ingredient interactions and baking techniques.

Careful attention to flour measurement and mixing techniques is essential to combat dryness in baked goods. Gradually incorporating flour into the batter and avoiding overmixing prevents excess gluten development, promoting a moist and tender texture. Experimenting with ingredient substitutions, such as adding yogurt or sour cream for added moisture, allows customization based on individual preferences. Conversely, reducing the liquid content and extending baking times can address excessive moisture issues.

In conclusion, baking is a captivating yet intricate journey filled with challenges that beckon bakers to unravel their secrets. From achieving the perfect texture and color to navigating the nuances of ingredient interactions, each challenge presents an opportunity for growth and mastery. Armed with knowledge, precision, and a touch of creativity, bakers can overcome these hurdles and embark on a delightful exploration of the art and science that is baking. By understanding the intricacies of the baking process, troubleshooting common challenges, and embracing the joy of

experimentation, bakers can elevate their skills and create a symphony of flavors and textures that captivate the senses and leave a lasting impression on those fortunate enough to savor their creations.

CHAPTER III

Classic Crinkles Unveiled

In-depth exploration of classic crinkle cookie recipes

The classic crinkle cookie, with its distinctive cracked appearance and irresistible fudgy interior, is a timeless favorite in the realm of baking. This delectable treat has a rich history, evolving over the years into a versatile canvas for creative variations while retaining its essential charm. An in-depth exploration of classic crinkle cookie recipes unveils the secrets behind their signature texture, flavor, and appearance, inviting bakers on a delightful journey into the heart of this beloved confection.

A harmonious blend of fundamental ingredients is at the core of any classic crinkle cookie recipe. The foundation begins with all-purpose flour, providing the structure that supports the cookie's characteristic cracks. Unsweetened cocoa powder, the key to the cookie's deep chocolate flavor, imparts a richness that captivates the senses. Leavening agents, typically baking powder, work with the dough's moisture content to create the perfect balance of a tender yet chewy crumb.

The role of fats in classic crinkle cookies is paramount, contributing to texture and flavor. With its creamy richness, butter is a common choice, infusing the cookies with a luxurious mouthfeel. The incorporation of brown sugar adds moisture, depth, and a hint of caramel undertones, enhancing the overall complexity of the cookie's taste profile. Eggs, with their binding properties, contribute structure while also providing a fudgy consistency to the interior.

Achieving the iconic cracked appearance of crinkle cookies results from a deliberate interplay between ingredients and baking techniques. Using granulated sugar, often rolled onto the cookie dough balls before baking, creates a sugary crust that contrasts beautifully with the dark chocolate interior. This coating contributes to the visual appeal and adds a delightful sweetness that complements the rich cocoa flavor.

The magic of classic crinkle cookies lies in the transformative process that occurs during baking. As the cookies spread and rise in the oven, the outer layer of sugar creates tension, causing the surface to crack and split. This phenomenon, coupled with the contrast in color between the dark cookie and the sugary cracks, produces the distinctive appearance that has made crinkle cookies a standout in the world of baked goods.

Beyond the foundational recipe, classic crinkle cookies invite creative interpretation and customization. Adding chocolate chips, chunks, or even white chocolate drizzles introduces delightful variations in texture and flavor. Nuts, such as walnuts or pecans, contribute a satisfying crunch that complements the cookie's fudgy interior. For those seeking an extra layer of complexity, a touch of espresso powder or cinnamon can elevate the chocolatey goodness to new heights.

Classic crinkle cookies are not confined to a single flavor profile. While the traditional chocolate version reigns supreme, bakers have explored various possibilities. Incorporating mint extract or peppermint candies introduces a refreshing twist reminiscent of a decadent chocolate mint treat. Orange zest or extract adds a citrusy brightness, offering a delightful contrast to the rich chocolate base.

The allure of classic crinkle cookies extends beyond their delectable taste and appearance; they are also a canvas for seasonal and thematic adaptations. During the festive holiday season, peppermint crinkle cookies adorned with crushed candy canes evoke a sense of winter cheer. In the warmth of summer, zesty citrus crinkle cookies bring a burst of sunshine to the dessert table. The versatility of the crinkle cookie recipe allows for endless exploration, ensuring a variation to suit every palate and occasion.

Baking classic crinkle cookies is not merely a culinary endeavor but a sensory experience that engages the senses from start to finish. The aroma wavers through the kitchen as the cookies bake, a tantalizing preview of the chocolatey bliss to come. The anticipation builds as the cookies emerge from the oven, their cracked surfaces glistening with sugar, promising a symphony of textures and flavors with every bite.

The pleasure of classic crinkle cookies extends to the ritual of their preparation. Rolling the cookie dough into balls and generously coating them in sugar becomes a tactile exploration, a hands-on connection to the alchemy of baking. The rhythmic process of placing the dough on the baking sheet and watching as it transforms into cracked perfection fosters a sense of accomplishment and joy that transcends the mere act of baking.

Classic crinkle cookies also hold a special place in the homemade gifts and shared moments tradition. A batch of freshly baked crinkle cookies, nestled in a charming tin or wrapped with care, becomes a heartfelt expression of warmth and generosity. Whether shared with loved ones during holiday gatherings, gifted to neighbors, or enjoyed as a sweet indulgence on a quiet afternoon, crinkle cookies can create moments of connection and delight. As with any classic recipe, the charm of crinkle cookies lies in their ability to evoke nostalgia while remaining eternally popular. They harken back to when simple ingredients came together to create extraordinary treats, and the joy of baking was a cherished tradition passed down through generations. Classic crinkle cookies serve as a delicious reminder of the enduring appeal of timeless recipes that bring comfort, joy, and a touch of magic to every kitchen they grace.

Step-by-step instructions for making the perfect crinkle

Embarking on the journey to create the perfect crinkle cookies is a delightful venture that promises to bring a symphony of flavors and textures to your kitchen. This step-by-step guide will navigate you through the artful process of crafting these timeless treats, ensuring that each batch emerges with the characteristic cracks, fudgy interior, and irresistible sweetness that define the perfect crinkle.

The journey begins with assembling the fundamental ingredients that form the foundation of crinkle cookie perfection. Gather all-purpose flour, unsweetened cocoa powder, baking powder, salt, unsalted butter, brown sugar, eggs, and vanilla extract in your culinary arsenal. These staples will lay the groundwork for a cookie that perfectly balances richness, sweetness, and a tender yet chewy texture.

Preheating your oven to the designated temperature, typically around 350°F (175°C). This ensures that your cookies bake evenly, achieving the desired texture and appearance. Take the time to bring the eggs and butter to room temperature; this facilitates smooth mixing and even incorporation of ingredients.

Sift together the all-purpose flour, unsweetened cocoa powder, baking powder, and a pinch of salt in a medium-sized bowl. Sifting removes any lumps and aerates the dry ingredients, contributing to a lighter texture in the final cookie.

In a separate large bowl, using a hand mixer or a stand mixer fitted with the paddle attachment, cream the room-temperature butter and brown sugar until light and fluffy. This process introduces air into the mixture, contributing to the tender crumb of the cookies.

Add the room-temperature eggs one at a time with the mixer on medium speed, allowing each to fully incorporate before adding the next. This step ensures a homogeneous mixture. Add a splash of pure vanilla extract, enhancing the cookies' flavor depth.

Gradually add the sifted dry ingredients to the wet mixture, mixing on low speed until just combined. It's crucial not to overmix at this stage to avoid excessive gluten development, leading to a tough texture. The goal is to achieve a cohesive dough with a consistent color.

Once the dough is well combined, cover the bowl with plastic wrap and refrigerate it for at least 1-2 hours. Chilling the dough serves multiple purposes—it solidifies the fats, prevents excessive spreading during baking, and allows the flavors to meld, enhancing the overall taste of the cookies.

Preheat your oven to 350°F (175°C) as the dough chills, and line your baking sheets with parchment paper. This helps with easy cleanup in addition to keeping the cookies from sticking.

After the chilling period, remove the dough from the refrigerator. Using your hands, roll the dough into uniform balls, approximately 1 to 1.5 inches in diameter. The balls' size influences the cookies' final appearance, so aim for consistency.

In a separate bowl, pour a generous amount of powdered sugar. Roll each dough ball in the powdered sugar until fully coated. The sugar coating not only contributes to the crinkle effect but also adds a delightful sweetness and texture to the exterior of the cookies.

Arrange the sugar-coated dough balls on the prepared baking sheets, leaving enough space between each for spreading during baking. The cookies will expand, and the cracks will develop during this process, creating the signature appearance of crinkle cookies.

Slide the baking sheets into the oven and bake the cookies for approximately 10-12 minutes. Keep a close eye on them, as baking times may vary depending on your oven and the size of the cookies. The goal is to set the edges while the centers remain slightly soft.

Once baked to perfection, allow the cookies to cool on the baking sheets for 5-7 minutes. This ensures that they set without becoming overly firm. The residual heat works its magic, contributing to the fudgy interior that distinguishes the perfect crinkle cookie.

After the initial cooling period on the baking sheets, carefully transfer the cookies to a wire cooling rack. This step allows for complete cooling and prevents residual heat from affecting the texture. Let the cookies cool completely before savoring their rich chocolate flavor.

Once your crinkle cookies have cooled, store them in an airtight container to maintain freshness. Whether you plan to enjoy them over a few days or share them with friends and family, proper storage ensures that each bite is as delightful as the first.

The beauty of the perfect crinkle cookie recipe lies in its adaptability. Feel free to experiment with additional mix-ins such as chocolate chips, nuts, or even a hint of spice. Consider exploring different flavor variations by incorporating extracts like peppermint or almond for a unique twist on the classic recipe.

With the baking process complete and the kitchen filled with the irresistible aroma of freshly baked crinkle cookies, the culmination has arrived. Savor each bite of the perfect crinkle—indulge in its fudgy interior, revel in the contrast of the sugary crust, and appreciate the simplicity and joy that a classic recipe can bring to your palate.

In conclusion, the step-by-step journey to crafting the perfect crinkle cookies is a testament to the art and science of baking. Every thorough process, selecting the components, forming them, and baking them, goes into making a dessert above and above the norm. As you embark on this culinary adventure, relish the process, take pride in the artistry of your creations, and share the joy of the perfect crinkle with those who appreciate the timeless allure of a classic cookie done to perfection.

Variations and creative twists on the classic recipe

The classic crinkle cookie, with its timeless combination of rich chocolate flavor, fudgy interior, and distinctive cracked appearance, is a versatile canvas for culinary creativity. While the traditional recipe holds a cherished place in the hearts of many, the beauty of crinkle cookies lies in their adaptability to various flavors, textures, and creative twists. Exploring the world of crinkle cookie variations opens the door to possibilities where bakers can infuse their unique flair into this beloved classic.

One delightful variation on the classic crinkle recipe involves the incorporation of additional textures through the addition of various mix-ins. Chocolate chips, whether dark, milk, or white, introduce pockets of gooey richness that complement the fudgy base. The juxtaposition of smooth chocolate chips against the soft crumb of the cookie creates a symphony of textures that elevates the overall indulgence. For those with a penchant for nuts, chopped walnuts, pecans, or hazelnuts offer a satisfying crunch, adding depth and complexity to each bite. This variation transforms the textural landscape of the crinkle cookie and allows for endless customization to suit individual preferences.

In flavor exploration, crinkle cookies welcome an array of creative twists that tantalize the taste buds. Peppermint extract introduces a refreshing and festive note, creating a chocolate mint delight perfect for the holiday season. The coolness of peppermint harmonizes with the rich cocoa, offering a refreshing contrast and a burst of flavor. Similarly, a hint of orange zest or a splash of citrus extract imparts a citrusy brightness that cuts through the chocolate richness, creating a decadent and refreshing cookie. These flavor variations expand the palate and lend a seasonal or thematic element to the classic crinkle, making it a versatile treat for various occasions.

For those who appreciate the allure of spices, incorporating cinnamon, nutmeg, or even a dash of cayenne pepper can introduce a layer of warmth and complexity to crinkle cookies. The subtle heat from spices like cayenne enhances the chocolatey notes, providing a sophisticated twist that appeals to adventurous palates. The aromatic warmth of cinnamon or nutmeg, on the other hand, adds a comforting element, making these spiced crinkle cookies perfect for cozy evenings and holiday gatherings. Experimenting with spices allows bakers to infuse the classic recipe with unexpected depth and nuance, transforming it into a unique and memorable experience.

A particularly indulgent variation of the classic crinkle involves the addition of gooey and decadent fillings. Imagine a crinkle cookie with a luscious caramel center or a pocket of smooth peanut butter hidden within its folds. These filled crinkle cookies surprise and delight with every bite, offering an extra layer of richness and complexity. Encasing a sweet surprise within the cookie dough requires a bit of finesse. Still, the payoff is a treat that transcends expectations, creating a sensory experience that combines the joy of discovery with the satisfaction of indulgence.

Furthermore, crinkle cookies provide a delightful platform for incorporating diverse and unconventional ingredients. Experimenting with unique add-ins such as dried fruits, shredded coconut, or crushed pretzels can yield unexpected and satisfying results. The interplay of sweet, salty, chewy, and crunchy adds a dynamic dimension to the classic crinkle, showcasing its adaptability and versatility. Infusing the dough with extracts like almond or coconut opens the door to exotic flavor profiles, offering a departure from the familiar while retaining the essence of the beloved cookie.

In the spirit of culinary innovation, some bakers take inspiration from popular desserts and treats to create crinkle cookie hybrids. The marriage of crinkle cookies with the flavors of s'mores, for instance, introduces graham cracker crumbs, marshmallow bits, and chocolate chips, capturing the essence of a classic campfire treat in every bite. Red velvet crinkle cookies, with their vibrant color and subtle cocoa flavor, pay homage to the beloved red velvet cake while maintaining the signature crinkle texture. These inventive variations showcase the versatility of crinkle cookies and celebrate the endless possibilities that arise when traditional recipes are reimagined with a creative twist.

For those with dietary preferences or restrictions, crinkle cookies can easily be adapted to accommodate various needs. Using gluten-free flour allows individuals with gluten sensitivities to indulge in the chocolatey goodness of crinkle cookies without compromise. Similarly, substituting plant-based ingredients such as coconut oil or a flaxseed egg for traditional dairy and eggs creates a vegan-friendly version of the classic treat. These adaptations cater to a broader audience and demonstrate the inclusive nature of crinkle cookies, ensuring that everyone can partake in the joy of this timeless confection.

The presentation of crinkle cookies also offers an opportunity for artistic expression. Rolling the cookie dough in colored sugars, vibrant sprinkles, or powdered freeze-dried fruit adds a visual dimension that enhances the overall appeal. This approach introduces a burst of color and allows bakers to customize crinkle cookies for specific occasions or themes. Whether creating a pastel palette for a springtime celebration or incorporating festive colors for holidays, the visual impact of crinkle cookies can be as captivating as their taste.

Moreover, the size and shape of crinkle cookies can be adjusted to suit individual preferences or to create a visual narrative. More minor, bite-sized crinkles are perfect for grazing and sharing, while more giant cookies make a bold statement and showcase the intricate cracks more prominently. Experimenting with cookie scoops, molding techniques, or even using cookie cutters for shaped crinkles adds more artistry to baking. These variations in presentation allow bakers to infuse their unique style into the classic crinkle, transforming it into a personalized work of edible art.

In conclusion, the world of crinkle cookies is one of endless possibilities, where the classic recipe serves as a springboard for creativity and innovation. Whether introducing new flavors, experimenting with textures, or taking inspiration from other beloved treats, crinkle cookies invite bakers to infuse their unique flair into this timeless confection. The beauty of crinkle cookies lies in their delectable taste and their adaptability and versatility, making them a beloved canvas for culinary exploration. So, embrace the art of variation, explore creative twists, and savor the joy of crinkle cookies in all their delightful forms.

CHAPTER IV

Sugar Sparkles Unleashed

Dive into the world of sugar sparkles and their variations.

Venturing into the enchanting realm of sugar sparkles opens a world of sweetness, elegance, and delightful confectionery artistry. These shimmering crystals, often adorning baked goods like cookies and pastries, are not merely a decorative touch but a testament to sugar's transformative power in its crystalline form. As we dive into the world of sugar sparkles, we uncover the various types, applications, and creative variations that elevate these tiny crystals into an essential element of the baker's palette.

At its core, sugar sparkles are crystallized sugar, a magical alchemy that turns ordinary granules into glistening crystals that catch and refract light. The process involves dissolving sugar in water, creating a supersaturated solution that, upon cooling, prompts the formation of crystals. When carefully grown and harvested, these crystals become the sparkles that adorn the surfaces of baked delights. The result is not just visual appeal but also a delicate crunch that adds texture and a touch of sweetness to the overall sensory experience.

One of the most iconic forms of sugar sparkles is sanding sugar. These large, coarse crystals come in vibrant colors, adding a dazzling finish to cookies, cupcakes, and pastries. With their bold, jewel-like appearance, sanding sugars create a visual spectacle that transforms ordinary treats into festive masterpieces. Whether sprinkled on top of sugar cookies, decorating the edges of cupcakes, or enhancing the allure of a fruit tart, sanding sugars brings a touch of glamour to the world of baking.

For a more refined and delicate touch, consider the elegance of pearl sugar. These petite, opaque pearls provide a subtle shimmer, resembling tiny droplets of dew on a morning blossom. Pearl sugar is often used to embellish pastries such as brioches, Danish pastries, and scones, creating a sophisticated presentation that appeals to both the eyes and the palate. The gentle sweetness of pearl sugar complements the buttery richness of pastries, offering a nuanced sweetness without overwhelming the overall flavor profile.

Beyond the traditional forms of sugar sparkles, creative bakers have explored myriad variations to infuse their creations with a personalized touch. Colored sugars, crafted by tinting granulated sugar with food-safe dyes, open a spectrum of possibilities for customizing desserts to suit various occasions and themes. Whether pastel hues for springtime celebrations, deep jewel tones for winter festivities, or vibrant primary colors for playful desserts, colored sugar sparkles allow for endless creativity in the kitchen.

Edible glitter, a dazzling innovation in the world of sugar sparkles, takes the art of decoration to new heights. Composed of food-grade coloring and either gum Arabic or sugar edible glitter, it transforms desserts into shimmering, magical creations. From fairy-tale-inspired cupcakes to celestial-themed cakes, edible glitter adds a touch of enchantment that captivates the imagination. The versatility of edible glitter extends beyond traditional baked goods, making it a whimsical choice for decorating beverages, chocolates, and even savory dishes, showcasing the boundless ways sugar sparkles can elevate culinary artistry.

Sugar sparkles, in their various forms, extend their influence beyond mere decoration; they play a pivotal role in enhancing the textural experience of baked goods. With their larger crystals, sanding sugars offer a satisfying crunch that contrasts with the tender crumbs of cookies or the flaky layers of pastries. This textural interplay elevates the overall enjoyment of a bite, turning a simple treat into a multisensory delight. Similarly, with its petite size and subtle sweetness, pearl sugar provides a delicate texture that complements the softness of breads and pastries, creating a harmonious balance that is as pleasing to the palate as it is to the eye.

The application of sugar sparkles is not limited to baked goods alone; they also play a starring role in candy-making. Rock candy, a crystallized form of sugar, showcases the natural beauty of sugar sparkles in its purest form. These crystalline formations, reminiscent of gemstones, are created through the slow evaporation of a sugar solution, resulting in large, faceted crystals. Rock candy serves as a sweet treat and a captivating visual spectacle that invites admiration. Growing rock candy at home has become a famous kitchen experiment, allowing enthusiasts to witness the mesmerizing transformation of sugar into crystalline beauty.

As we explore the diverse world of sugar sparkles, we must recognize their cultural significance and historical roots. Sugar, once a rare and precious commodity, evolved from being a luxury enjoyed by the elite to becoming a ubiquitous staple in kitchens worldwide. The art of sugar crafting, including the creation of sparkles, has deep historical roots in European and Middle Eastern culinary traditions. From the delicate sugar sculptures of Renaissance Europe to the intricate sugar work of the Ottoman Empire, sugar has been molded, crystallized, and transformed into edible art for centuries.

In modern times, the accessibility of sugar sparkles has democratized the art of decorating, allowing homebakers to infuse their creations with a touch of glamour. Whether sprinkling sanding sugar on holiday cookies, embellishing birthday cakes with edible glitter, or experimenting with colored sugars for everyday treats, home bakers can channel their creativity to elevate desserts into edible masterpieces. The versatility of sugar sparkles aligns with the evolving landscape of baking, where the intersection of tradition and innovation gives rise to delightful expressions of culinary art.

The cultural significance of sugar sparkles also extends to festive traditions and celebrations. In many cultures, decorating sweets with sugar sparkles is intertwined with joyous occasions and special festivities. From the colorful sanding sugars adorning Mardi Gras King Cakes to the delicate pearl sugar gracing Scandinavian holiday pastries, sugar sparkles are integral to the culinary narrative accompanying cherished traditions. The visual impact of these sparkles enhances the celebratory atmosphere, turning desserts into symbolic expressions of joy, abundance, and festivity.

As we delve into the world of sugar sparkles, it's worth noting their role in the art of presentation. The visual allure of desserts, often the first sensory encounter with a dish, sets the stage for the following culinary experience. With their ability to catch and reflect light, sugar sparkles transform ordinary treats into extraordinary creations. A simple sugar cookie, when adorned with an artful sprinkle of colored sugars, becomes a work of edible art that beckons with its visual charm. The presentation of desserts, guided by the strategic use of sugar sparkles, invites anticipation, heightens the dining experience, and contributes to the overall pleasure derived from indulging in sweet delights.

Sugar sparkles continue to evolve in the modern culinary landscape, where innovation and experimentation are celebrated. The rise of plant-based and natural alternatives has spurred the development of sparkles made from ingredients such as agave nectar, beet sugar, or natural fruit extracts. These alternatives not only cater to dietary preferences but also align with the growing demand for natural, transparent ingredients in baking. As sugar sparkles adapt to changing tastes and preferences, they retain their timeless appeal as a medium for artistic expression in the realm of sweets.

In conclusion, the world of sugar sparkles is a captivating journey into the artful interplay of sweetness, light, and creativity. From the historical roots of sugar crafting to the modern innovations that continue to shape its evolution, sugar sparkles have transcended their decorative role to become an integral part of the culinary experience. Whether adorning classic cookies, enhancing the visual spectacle of candies, or contributing to the art of presentation, sugar sparkles weave a tale of sweetness that engages the senses and brings joy to the heart. As we embrace the diverse forms and variations of sugar sparkles, we celebrate not just the culinary craft but also the cultural richness and artistic expression that sugar, in its crystalline splendor, brings to the world of sweets.

Unique ingredients and flavor combinations

The realm of culinary creativity is a vast and ever-expanding landscape, with chefs and home cooks constantly seeking to push the boundaries of flavor and texture. At the heart of this exploration lies unique ingredients and the artful pairing of flavor combinations, transforming ordinary dishes into extraordinary culinary experiences. Infusing unexpected elements, exotic spices, and novel ingredients into traditional recipes opens a world of possibilities, inviting adventurous palates to embark on a journey of sensory delight.

One avenue of culinary innovation involves incorporating unique and unconventional ingredients that add a distinctive flair to dishes. From ancient grains and heirloom vegetables to foraged herbs and exotic fruits, exploring diverse ingredients introduces a depth of flavor and a richness of texture that captivates the palate. Consider quinoa's nutty and wholesome profile, an ancient grain celebrated for its protein content and versatility. Whether used in salads, pilafs, or as a base for protein bowls, quinoa brings a satisfying chewiness and a subtle earthiness that elevates various dishes.

Heirloom varieties shine as culinary gems in the realm of vegetables, each boasting a unique taste and vibrant color palette. From the sweet, golden hues of heirloom tomatoes to the earthy, multicolored tones of heirloom carrots, these vegetables contribute visual appeal and offer nuanced flavors beyond the standard supermarket varieties. Using heirloom vegetables allows for a heightened appreciation of the diversity within the plant kingdom, adding a layer of sophistication to dishes and celebrating the rich tapestry of nature's bounty.

Foraging, once a practice reserved for seasoned experts, has become mainstream culinary consciousness. Wildcrafted ingredients, gathered from forests, meadows, and coastlines, bring an element of surprise and connection to the natural world. Wild mushrooms, such as morels or chanterelles, impart an earthy and umami-rich essence to dishes. At the same time, edible flowers like violets or nasturtiums add a delicate floral note that enhances a plate's visual and gustatory aspects. Including foraged ingredients reflects a return to a more intimate and sustainable approach to sourcing, connecting the diner to the landscape in which their food originates.

In the world of fruits, exotic varieties offer a burst of tropical vibrancy and an array of complex flavors. With its striking pink exterior and speckled interior, Dragon fruit adds a subtle sweetness and a visually stunning element to salads and desserts. The creamy and custard-like flesh of cherimoya, often called the "custard apple," introduces a tropical indulgence that pairs well with sweet and savory preparations. These exotic fruits contribute to the diversity of taste experiences but also serve as a reminder of the vast botanical treasures waiting to be explored.

The spice cabinet, a treasure trove of aromatic wonders, is pivotal in creating unique and memorable flavor combinations. Although commonplace spices like paprika, cumin, and cinnamon are adored for their well-known flavors, lesser-known spices give recipes a touch of mystery. With its tart and citrusy notes, Sumac brightens dishes with a burst of acidity. At the same time, za'atar, a Middle Eastern spice blend, introduces a medley of herbs, sesame seeds, and Sumac for a complex and savory flavor profile. The judicious use of these unique spices transforms ordinary dishes into culinary masterpieces, transporting the palate to far-flung regions and cultures. The fusion of global cuisines has become a hallmark of contemporary culinary innovation, giving rise to unexpected flavor combinations that challenge and delight the taste buds. The marriage of sweet and savory, a juxtaposition common in many international cuisines, creates a symphony of flavors that transcends traditional boundaries. Consider the classic pairing of prosciutto and melon, where the salty richness of cured ham meets the juicy sweetness of ripe cantaloupe, resulting in a harmonious and refreshing melody on the palate. Similarly, including fruits like mango or pineapple in savory dishes adds a tropical brightness that complements the delicious components, exemplifying the art of balance and contrast in flavor pairing.

Exploring the realm of umami, the savory and profoundly satisfying fifth taste, opens avenues for creating complex and layered flavor profiles. Ingredients rich in umami, such as miso paste, seaweed, and fermented soy products like tamari or soy sauce, contribute depth and a savory richness to dishes. Incorporating umami-rich elements goes beyond traditional savory applications, finding a place in desserts and cocktails, where the nuanced complexity enhances sweetness and adds a sophisticated edge to the overall flavor experience.

The rise of plant-based and alternative proteins has introduced a new dimension to culinary creativity, challenging preconceived notions of flavor and texture. Ingredients like jackfruit, with its fibrous and meaty texture, serve as a versatile canvas for absorbing myriad flavors, making it a popular choice for plant-based tacos, curries, and sandwiches. Similarly, tempeh, a fermented soy product, brings a hearty and nutty profile that stands up well to bold marinades and spices. These plant-based alternatives cater to dietary preferences and contribute to a more sustainable and inclusive approach to gastronomy.

The exploration of fermentation, a time-honored culinary technique, introduces a world of complex and tangy flavors that add depth and character to dishes. Fermented vegetables, such as sauerkraut or kimchi, provide a piquant and probiotic-rich element that brightens and revitalizes both simple and elaborate preparations. Fermented condiments like miso and gochujang, with their umami-laden intensity, serve as flavor enhancers that elevate the overall taste profile of a dish. Once relegated to traditional preservation methods, the art of fermentation has become a source of culinary inspiration, fostering a revival of ancient practices and a renaissance of bold and dynamic flavors.

The artful combination of sweet and savory extends to desserts, where pastry chefs experiment with unexpected pairings to create memorable confections. Incorporating herbs such as thyme or basil into desserts adds a fresh and aromatic element that complements the sweetness, while floral infusions like lavender or rosewater introduce a subtle perfume that elevates the sensory experience. Including savory elements, such as olive oil or balsamic reduction, in desserts like ice creams or cakes creates a nuanced sweetness that defies conventional expectations, resulting in both familiar and intriguing desserts.

Beyond the traditional flavor categories of sweet, savory, salty, sour, and umami, culinary experimentation has given rise to unexpected combinations that challenge the conventional palate. The infusion of smoke, a technique traditionally associated with savory barbecue, finds its way into desserts, imparting a subtle smokiness that adds complexity and depth. Incorporating floral elements, such as hibiscus or elderflower, introduces a delicate and aromatic quality that transforms beverages, desserts, and even savory dishes into sensory experiences reminiscent of blooming gardens and fragrant meadows.

In the world of artisanal and craft products, the use of unique and unconventional ingredients has become a defining characteristic. Craft chocolatiers, for example, explore single-origin cacao beans, rare varieties, and innovative inclusions to create chocolates that showcase the terroir of the cacao and push the boundaries of flavor exploration. Infusions of botanicals, spices, and even savory elements like sea salt or smoked paprika create chocolates beyond mere confectionery, becoming expressions of culinary art.

In conclusion, using unique ingredients and flavor combinations is a testament to the ever-evolving nature of culinary exploration. From ancient grains and foraged delicacies to exotic spices and unexpected pairings, the culinary landscape is a canvas waiting to be painted with bold strokes of creativity. As chefs and home cooks continue to push boundaries, challenge expectations, and embrace the diversity of flavors offered by nature, the world of gastronomy becomes a vibrant tapestry of taste, texture, and sensory delight. The exploration of unique ingredients and flavor combinations reflects the dynamic evolution of culinary arts and invites us to savor the boundless possibilities that arise when we open our palates to the wonders of the culinary world.

Decorating techniques for sugar sparkles

The art of decorating with sugar sparkles transcends the boundaries of culinary craftsmanship, evolving into edible artistry that elevates desserts to new heights of visual delight. The techniques employed in adorning confections with these glistening crystals are as diverse as the sparkles, allowing pastry chefs and home bakers alike to unleash their creativity and transform ordinary treats into extraordinary masterpieces.

The simple sprinkle is one of the most classic and widely used techniques for decorating with sugar sparkles. This approach involves generously dusting or sprinkling the sparkles onto the surface of baked goods, creating a magical and enchanting effect. Whether adorning cookies, cupcakes, or cakes, the sprinkle technique allows for a quick and effortless application that adds instant glamour. The versatility of this method is apparent in its ability to create both subtle accents and bold statements, depending on the quantity and distribution of the sparkles. The sprinkle technique is prevalent for sugar cookies, where the sparkles adhere to the surface, creating a dazzling finish that showcases the contours of the cookie.

The painting technique offers precision and artistic flair for a more refined and controlled application of sugar sparkles. This method involves using a food-safe brush to delicately paint or dust the sparkles onto specific areas of a dessert, allowing for intricate designs and detailed patterns. Pastry chefs often employ this technique when crafting elegant pastries, such as éclairs, where the controlled placement of sparkles adds a touch of sophistication. The painting technique also contributes to creating edible illustrations or designs on cookies, providing a canvas for edible art that captivates the eye.

Embossing or imprinting sparkles onto the surface of desserts introduces a textured and tactile dimension to the decoration. This technique is achieved by pressing sugar sparkles into the surface of soft or pliable confections before they set. Pastry chefs may use specialized stamps, molds, or even freehand techniques to create patterns or motifs directly on the surface of fondant, marzipan, or other pliable mediums. The embossing technique seamlessly integrates sparkles into the desert, creating a polished and professional appearance. This method is often employed in making wedding or special occasion cakes, where the intricate detailing enhances the overall visual impact.

The layering technique involves building up multiple layers of sugar sparkles to create a textured and multidimensional effect. This method is particularly effective for adding depth and complexity to larger surfaces, such as the icing on a cake. By applying layers of sparkles in varying shades or colors, bakers can achieve a gradient or ombre effect that transitions seamlessly across the dessert. The layering technique also allows for creating elaborate and eye-catching designs, as each layer of sparkles contributes to the overall visual impact. The layering technique adds intricacy and sophistication to the decoration, whether creating a cascading effect on a tiered cake or a gradient on a single-layer confection.

Incorporating sugar sparkles into icing or frosting provides a smooth and seamless integration of these edible crystals into the overall design of a dessert. This technique is achieved by mixing sugar sparkles directly into the icing or frosting, creating a glittering and cohesive finish. Whether applied as a thin glaze or a thick layer of frosting, the incorporation of sparkles into icing imparts a shimmering quality that transforms the entire surface of a dessert. This technique is popularized in cupcakes, where the icing acts as a medium for the glitter, covering the whole top of the dessert with a coating of delectable sparkles.

Beyond traditional application techniques, using stencils introduces precision and detail, allowing for intricate and customized designs. Pastry chefs and home bakers can employ stencils made of food-safe materials to create specific patterns or images on the surface of desserts. Intricate designs emerge with a professional and polished finish by placing the stencil over the dessert and then dusting or sprinkling sugar sparkles onto the exposed areas. Using stencils to decorate cookies is popular because they allow you to choose how much sparkle is applied to create detailed patterns that transform each cookie into an edible piece of art.

The crystalline texture of sugar sparkles also creates textured effects on desserts. By applying sparkles in a deliberate and patterned manner, bakers can craft surfaces that mimic the appearance of frosted or crystallized textures. This technique is often used for winter-themed desserts, where the sparkle of snow or frost is replicated on the surface of cakes, cookies, or cupcakes. The textured effect adds a tactile and visual element that enhances the theme and narrative of the dessert, transporting the observer to a winter wonderland of edible enchantment.

For those seeking to make a bold and dramatic statement, the dip or roll technique offers a striking and full-coverage application of sugar sparkles. This method involves dipping the entire surface of a dessert or a portion of it into a bowl or container filled with sugar sparkles, ensuring complete coverage. The dip or roll technique is commonly used for items like cake pops or chocolate-covered strawberries, where the sparkles adhere to the outer layer of icing or chocolate. The result is a confection encased in a layer of edible brilliance, creating a visually stunning and impactful treat.

Using sugar sparkles with other decorative elements, such as edible flowers, metallic leaves, or fondant cutouts, allows for creating elaborate and multidimensional designs. By strategically combining various decorative elements, bakers can craft desserts that are not only visually stunning but also tell a story or convey a theme. Whether adorning a wedding cake with delicate fondant lace and sparkles or embellishing cupcakes with edible flowers and glitter, the combination of elements adds depth and interest to the overall design, creating a dessert that is as captivating as it is delicious.

In conclusion, the decorating techniques for sugar sparkles are as diverse and dynamic as the world of culinary creativity itself. From the classic sprinkle to the intricate painting, embossing, layering, and beyond, each technique offers a unique approach to incorporating these edible crystals into desserts. Whether aiming for simplicity or complexity, precision or whimsy, the use of sugar sparkles in decorating allows for a level of customization and artistry that transforms every treat into a canvas for edible expression. As bakers continue to explore and innovate, sugar sparkle decoration remains a realm of endless possibilities, inviting professionals and home enthusiasts to infuse their creations with the magic and allure of edible brilliance.

CHAPTER V

Nostalgia in Every Bite

The emotional connection to classic cookies

The emotional connection to classic cookies transcends the realm of mere culinary enjoyment, reaching into the deep recesses of our memories, traditions, and shared experiences. These timeless treats, with their familiar flavors and comforting aromas, hold a unique place in the hearts of individuals across generations. More than a simple confection, classic cookies serve as vessels for emotions, nostalgia, and the intangible threads that weave the fabric of our lives.

The power to evoke cherished memories is at the heart of the emotional connection to classic cookies. The mere scent of cookies baking in the oven can trigger a cascade of recollections, transporting individuals to the warmth of childhood kitchens and the embrace of familial love. Baking cookies with parents or grandparents becomes a shared experience that evolves into the tapestry of one's memory, forging a connection between the comforting aroma of baking dough and the safety of home. In these moments, cookies become more than a culinary creation; they become a tangible link to the past, a conduit for reliving moments of joy and togetherness.

Moreover, the emotional tie to classic cookies is intricately entwined with the concept of tradition and ritual. Baking cookies, especially using time-honored recipes passed down through generations, becomes a ritual that transcends the kitchen. A familial tradition imparts a sense of continuity and connection to the past. Following a familiar recipe, measuring out ingredients, and carefully shaping each cookie are not just culinary actions but a ceremonial dance that reinforces a sense of familial identity. These cookies symbolize the shared history and enduring bonds that define a family.

Furthermore, classic cookies serve as tokens of love and care, extending the emotional connection beyond the kitchen to become gestures of affection. Baking and sharing cookies become a way of expressing love, gratitude, or support. Whether presented as a homemade gift to a friend, a plate of cookies to welcome new neighbors, or a batch baked to comfort someone in need, classic cookies become a medium through which emotions are communicated. Offering a freshly baked cookie becomes a universal language of kindness and nurturing, fostering a sense of connection and community.

Classic cookies provide solace and a sense of normalcy in celebration or sorrow. During festive occasions, the appearance of holiday cookies or special treats becomes synonymous with joy and merriment. The familiar flavors and shapes associated with these celebratory cookies contribute to the festive atmosphere, creating a sensory experience inseparable from the joyous occasion. Conversely, baking or enjoying a favorite cookie can offer a brief respite from life's challenges in moments of sadness or difficulty, providing comfort and a temporary escape into the realm of sweetness.

The emotional connection to classic cookies is also intertwined with the concept of indulgence and self-care. Amid the demands of daily life, taking a moment to savor a warm, freshly baked cookie becomes an act of self-nurturing. The combination of flavors and textures, the familiar embrace of a favorite recipe, and the sensory pleasure derived from each bite create a moment of respite and enjoyment. Treating oneself to a cookie, whether paired with a cup of tea on a quiet afternoon or enjoyed as a midnight snack, becomes a form of self- care —a small, edible indulgence that brings comfort and joy to the individual.

Moreover, classic cookies often serve as carriers of cultural and familial heritage, carrying within them the stories and traditions of generations past. Recipes passed down from grandparents or rooted in cultural practices become a tangible link to ancestral roots. Baking and sharing these cookies becomes a way of preserving cultural identity and passing on culinary knowledge to the next generation. Classic cookies, shaped into intricate forms with cultural significance or flavored with ingredients emblematic of a particular heritage, become vessels through which stories are shared, and traditions are perpetuated.

Classic cookies hold collective significance in the broader cultural context, symbolizing shared experiences and communal rituals. From the iconic chocolate chip cookie to the beloved snickerdoodle, these treats are often woven into cultural celebrations, traditions, and shared moments. The cookie jar, a familiar fixture in many households, becomes a repository of sugary delights, shared memories, and communal enjoyment. They are offering cookies to guests, whether as a welcoming gesture or a token of hospitality, becomes a universal expression of sharing and connection.

In the realm of nostalgia, classic cookies evoke a longing for simpler times and the innocence of childhood. The scent of cookies baking in the oven or the taste of a familiar recipe can transport individuals back to a moment when life seemed less complicated and the world more welcoming. The emotional pull of nostalgia is particularly potent in classic cookies, where the sensory experiences associated with these treats become intertwined with the emotions and perceptions of a bygone era. Biting into a cookie can become a journey back in time, a brief respite in the present to relish the flavors and emotions of the past.

The emotional connection to classic cookies is not only about the past but also about the present moment and the simple joys it can bring. In a world of complexity and uncertainty, baking or enjoying a cookie becomes a grounding and accessible source of happiness. The sensory pleasures derived from the crunch of a perfectly baked cookie, the melt-in-your-mouth texture, and the balance of sweet and savory flavors create a moment of pure, unadulterated joy. In their simplicity, classic cookies become a source of delight that transcends age, background, and circumstance.

In conclusion, the emotional connection to classic cookies is a multi-faceted and profoundly resonant experience that extends beyond culinary pleasure. These simple treats serve as vessels for memories, traditions, and expressions of love. They become conduits for cultural heritage, symbols of celebration and solace, and gateways to the past through the lens of nostalgia. Whether shared with loved ones, enjoyed as a personal indulgence, or offered as a gesture of kindness, classic cookies embody the universal language of joy and connection. In a world where moments of genuine comfort and happiness are treasured, traditional cookies stand as timeless ambassadors of the emotional richness found in the simplest pleasures.

Stories and memories associated with these treats

Classic treats, whether they take the form of Grandma's apple pie, Mom's chocolate chip cookies, or the cherished brownies from a childhood friend, are not merely culinary delights; they are vessels of stories and memories that weave the tapestry of our lives. Each bite into these timeless treats carries the weight of shared experiences, the laughter of gatherings, and the warmth of familial bonds. The stories and memories associated with these treats become a living narrative, a collection of moments frozen in time, waiting to be relived with each nostalgic taste.

These treats are more than the sum of their ingredients; they are repositories of personal and collective histories. Take, for example, the chocolate chip cookie, a staple in many households. Each batch holds a story—perhaps the tale of a grandmother who, during a bygone era, ingeniously substituted broken chocolate bars for baker's chocolate, inadvertently giving birth to an American classic. The recipe's simplicity belies the complexity of its narratives: the laughter in the kitchen, the familial bonds forged over a shared love of sweets, and the passing down of a cherished tradition from one generation to the next.

Beyond the family circle, these treats often symbolize friendship and shared experiences. Consider the iconic brownie baked for a school bake sale or as a gesture of comfort for a friend going through a tough time. The memories associated with these treats extend beyond the kitchen, intertwining with the stories of friendships formed, challenges faced, and triumphs celebrated. Sharing a plate of brownies becomes a symbol of camaraderie, a gesture that transcends mere sustenance to become a tangible expression of care and support.

Moreover, these treats become woven into the fabric of cultural and societal narratives. Holiday tables are graced by pies, cakes, and cookies that carry the weight of tradition and collective memory. The Thanksgiving pumpkin pie, the Christmas fruitcake, or the Hanukkah sufganiyot have a story rooted in cultural heritage. These treats provide a sensory experience and serve as markers of cultural identity, connecting individuals to their roots and the larger narrative of shared traditions.

Baking becomes a storytelling medium, with each recipe representing a chapter in the book of one's culinary journey. The kitchen becomes a stage where stories unfold; the clinking of measuring spoons and the whirring of mixers create a symphony of memories. The missteps and triumphs in the kitchen become chapters of resilience, resourcefulness, and sometimes hilarity as generations pass down recipes and the tales of the culinary adventures that accompany them.

Moreover, these treats often become associated with pivotal moments in life. A birthday cake symbolizes another year of growth and celebration, and the blowing out of candles becomes a ritual that marks the passage of time. Wedding cakes, adorned with layers of fondant and intricate designs, become more than a confection; they become symbols of love, commitment, and the beginning of a shared journey. These treats anchor themselves in our memories, becoming witnesses to significant moments but active participants in the emotional landscape of our lives.

Recreating these treats can be a form of time travel, allowing individuals to revisit the stories and emotions associated with specific moments. A whiff of freshly baked cinnamon rolls can transport someone back to lazy Sunday mornings, where the aroma permeated the kitchen and signaled a day of relaxation and indulgence. The taste of a childhood favorite, like Rice Krispies treats or peanut butter cookies, can trigger a flood of memories—the school lunches, the after-school snacks, and the joy of discovering a treat waiting at home.

Beyond personal narratives, these treats often carry cultural and societal stories, acting as time capsules that encapsulate the flavors and trends of a particular era. For example, the gelatin salads and molded desserts of the mid-20th century speak to the culinary preferences and influences of that time. The rise of gluten-free, vegan, or keto-friendly treats in recent years reflects not just dietary trends but societal shifts toward wellness and inclusivity. These treats become artifacts, telling tales of changing tastes, evolving values, and the ever-shifting landscape of the culinary world.

Furthermore, these treats often become vehicles for storytelling in a broader sense, with cookbooks and culinary blogs serving as platforms for sharing narratives and recipes. The stories behind a dish—its cultural roots, the inspiration behind its creation, or the memories it evokes—add depth and richness to the culinary experience. Cooks and bakers become storytellers, weaving narratives that extend beyond the kitchen and into the hearts of those who partake in their creations.

In conclusion, classic treats are not just about taste and texture but about the stories and memories they carry. From the chocolate chip cookies of family gatherings to the birthday cakes marking milestones, each treat becomes a chapter in the autobiography of our lives. The kitchen transforms into a stage where stories unfold, and the act of baking becomes a form of storytelling. These treats represent shared experiences, familial bonds, and cultural heritage. As we savor each bite, we don't just taste the ingredients—we taste the laughter, the celebrations, and the stories that make these treats timeless companions in life's journey.

Creating new memories with classic crinkles and sugar sparkles

Creating new memories with classic crinkles and sugar sparkles is a delightful journey into taste, tradition, and the joyous art of baking. These iconic treats, with their distinct textures and sparkling allure, not only transport us to cherished moments of the past but also invite us to forge new memories, weaving the magic of the kitchen into the fabric of our lives.

Classic crinkles, with their crackled surfaces and soft centers, evoke the nostalgia of family gatherings and holiday celebrations. Biting into a chocolate crinkle cookie, dusted with a snowy layer of powdered sugar, can transport us to winter afternoons spent in the warm glow of the kitchen. The memories of rolling dough into small balls, eagerly awaiting the transformation in the oven and the joy of seeing the crinkles emerge—all these experiences become the ingredients of a timeless recipe for creating new memories.

Sugar sparkles, those glistening crystals that add a touch of magic to baked goods, serve as the edible fairy dust in this memory-making journey. Whether delicately adorning a sugar cookie or creating a dazzling spectacle on a cake, sugar sparkles infuse each creation with a sprinkle of enchantment. As we decorate, the kitchen becomes a canvas, and applying sugar sparkles becomes a form of edible artistry—an opportunity to unleash creativity and craft treats that are not only delicious but visually captivating.

The process of creating new memories with classic crinkles and sugar sparkles often begins with the gathering of loved ones in the kitchen. The rhythmic sound of measuring ingredients, the laughter shared over mixing bowls, and the anticipation of tasting the finished creations contribute to the communal experience. During these times, the kitchen becomes a haven where friendships are forged, relationships are developed, and baking fosters community.

The aroma of classic crinkles wafting through the kitchen is not just a sensory delight but the scent of memories in the making. The warm, comforting fragrance triggers a cascade of emotions, inviting us to be fully present in the moment. As we watch the crinkles form in the oven and see the cookies emerge with their distinct patterns, each batch becomes a testament to the beauty of transformation—a metaphor for how moments evolve into memories.

Decorating with sugar sparkles is a celebration of creativity and individual expression. From the meticulous painting of intricate designs to the playful sprinkle of crystals, each cookie or cake becomes a unique work of art. This decoration process is not just about aesthetics; it is an opportunity to infuse personal touches, tell stories through edible designs, and leave a signature of individuality on each treat. The shared experience of decorating, whether with family, friends, or even alone, becomes a space for self-expression and creating edible masterpieces.

Moreover, classic crinkles and sugar sparkles become vehicles for celebration and joy. Birthdays adorned with crinkle-topped cupcakes or holiday gatherings featuring a sparkling array of cookies—these treats can elevate ordinary moments into extraordinary celebrations. Presenting these creations becomes a gesture of love and a way to express care for those we hold dear. In the exchange of treats, we exchange sentiments of joy, gratitude, and the sweetness of shared experiences. When

we provide these sweets to people as presents or get-togethers, we invite them to make memories with us. Offering a homemade crinkle or a sugar-sparked delight becomes a bridge between the giver and the receiver—a shared experience beyond the physical gift. The recipient tastes the flavors and receives a piece of the baker's heart, infused with the care and intentionality that went into creating the treat.

Furthermore, introducing classic crinkles and sugar sparkles to a new generation becomes a form of culinary storytelling. Passing down recipes, demonstrating decorating techniques, and sharing the stories behind these treats become a way to connect with family heritage. In this context, the kitchen becomes a classroom where traditions are taught, and the baton of culinary knowledge is passed from generation to generation. In their timelessness, classic crinkles and sugar sparkles become bridges that span across generations, connecting the past with the present and paving the way for future memories.

In the era of social media and digital storytelling, classic crinkles, and sugar sparkles find a new stage for their performances. Baking and decorating become a shareable narrative, documented through photos, videos, and captions. In this virtual realm, the joy of creating memories extends beyond the immediate circle of family and friends to a global community of bakers and food enthusiasts. The online space becomes a gallery where individuals showcase their creations, exchange ideas, and inspire others to embark on their memory-making journeys.

Beyond the act of baking, classic crinkles, and sugar sparkles become integral to the rituals of holidays and special occasions. The presence of these treats on the dessert table signals the arrival of festivities and adds a touch of tradition to the celebration. Whether it's the anticipation of the first bite into a crinkle on Christmas morning or the awe-inspired gaze at a cake adorned with sparkles on a birthday, these treats become a tangible part of the rituals that define our cultural and personal calendars.

In conclusion, creating new memories with classic crinkles and sugar sparkles celebrates taste, tradition, and the profound joy of baking. From the initial gathering of ingredients to the final presentation of decorated treats, each step becomes a chapter in the story of memory-making. With their ability to evoke nostalgia and infuse joy into shared experiences, these iconic treats become more than just desserts—they become companions in creating and savoring the moments that make life sweet. As we engage in the delightful dance of baking, decorating, and sharing, we weave a tapestry of memories that will be cherished and recounted with the same warmth and delight as the treats.

CHAPTER VI

Gluten-Free and Vegan Options

Adapting classic recipes for dietary preferences

Adapting classic recipes for dietary preferences is a culinary art that marries tradition with innovation, catering to the diverse tapestry of tastes and nutritional needs that characterize contemporary lifestyles. In the evolving landscape of dietary choices, the classic recipes that once adorned family tables and shaped cultural culinary identities are transforming to accommodate a spectrum of preferences, ranging from vegetarian and vegan lifestyles to gluten-free and keto diets. This adaptation not only reflects a sensitivity to the varied dietary needs of individuals but also breathes new life into time-honored dishes, ensuring their continued relevance and enjoyment across a broad spectrum of palates.

Adapting classic recipes begins with a thoughtful examination of the ingredients that form the backbone of these culinary traditions. For instance, with its rich flavors and savory depth, the traditional meat-based Bolognese sauce can undergo a vegetarian metamorphosis by replacing the meat with a medley of hearty vegetables or plant-based protein alternatives. This alteration aligns the dish with vegetarian preferences and introduces a vibrant array of colors and textures, enhancing the visual and gustatory appeal. The adaptation process becomes a dance of flavors, where the essence of the original recipe is retained while embracing the nuances of plant-based alternatives.

In baking, the adaptation journey turns toward the gluten-free or keto-friendly path. Flour, a fundamental ingredient in classic recipes like cakes, cookies, and bread, becomes a canvas for experimentation. Almond flour, coconut flour, and other grain-free alternatives step into the spotlight, offering a gluten-free option for those with dietary restrictions and imparting a unique texture and flavor profile to the baked goods. The art of adapting involves striking a delicate balance between maintaining the structural integrity of the dish and exploring the creative possibilities that alternative flours bring to the table.

Vegan adaptations of classic recipes often involve reimagining the role of dairy and eggs, integral components in traditional cooking. In the quest for plant-based alternatives, coconut, almond, and soy milk emerge as substitutes for dairy, adding a luscious creaminess to dishes without compromising flavor. Meanwhile, when combined with water, the humble flaxseed or chia seed transforms into a gelatinous binder that stands in for eggs, ensuring the cohesion of batters and doughs. These substitutions accommodate vegan dietary preferences and contribute to the evolution of a more sustainable and plant-centric culinary landscape. The adaptation journey is about replacing ingredients and embracing a mindset that encourages exploration and creativity. Once relegated to the sidelines as a humble vegetable, Cauliflower steps into the limelight as a versatile substitute for grains, creating a low-carb alternative for rice or pizza crust. Spiralized zucchini takes on the role of pasta, offering a nutrient-dense option for those seeking lighter alternatives. The culinary canvas expands as adaptors experiment with unconventional ingredients, elevating classic recipes to new heights of innovation while maintaining a deep respect for the origins and flavors that define these dishes.

As the dietary landscape diversifies, the adaptation of classic recipes extends beyond ingredient substitutions to address broader nutritional considerations. The rise of the keto diet, characterized by a low-carbohydrate and high-fat approach, prompts adaptations emphasizing healthy fats and lean proteins. Avocado has become a star player, lending its creamy texture to desserts and dips while contributing heart-healthy monounsaturated fats. Nuts and seeds, with their nutritional richness, find a prominent place in adaptations that align with the principles of the keto lifestyle, offering a satisfying crunch and a nutrient boost.

Moreover, adapting classic recipes responds to the growing awareness of food allergies and sensitivities, ensuring that individuals with specific dietary needs can partake in the joys of iconic dishes. Gluten-free adaptations, for instance, enable those with celiac disease or gluten intolerance to savor the pleasures of pizza, pasta, and baked goods without worrying about adverse reactions. The lactose-intolerant finds solace in dairy-free renditions of creamy sauces and decadent desserts, showcasing that dietary restrictions need not sacrifice flavor or indulgence.

Adapting classic recipes, the culinary landscape becomes a stage for inclusivity, where diverse dietary preferences coexist harmoniously. The adaptors, whether home cooks, professional chefs, or food entrepreneurs, become ambassadors of a gastronomic movement that embraces the kaleidoscope of tastes and dietary choices. This movement transcends the notion of restriction, transforming it into an opportunity for exploration and discovery, where every adaptation celebrates culinary diversity.

In cultural cuisines, adaptation becomes a bridge between tradition and innovation. Take, for instance, the traditional Indian butter chicken dish, a creamy and flavorful delight loved globally. Adapting this classic to a plant-based, vegan version involves replacing chicken with tofu or plant-based protein alternatives and dairy with coconut milk or cashew cream. The result is a dish that not only caters to the dietary preferences of vegans but also introduces a fresh perspective on a beloved cultural icon, illustrating how adaptation can breathe new life into traditional recipes while honoring their cultural roots.

The adaptability of classic recipes is most evident in the ever-expanding world of plant-based alternatives. Burgers crafted from mushrooms, lentils, or black beans challenge the traditional meat-centric narrative, offering a savory and satisfying experience that appeals to vegetarians and those seeking more sustainable food choices. Plant-based sausages, made from a medley of vegetables and protein-rich grains, redefine the notion of a classic BBQ, showcasing that the essence of beloved dishes can endure even as the ingredients evolve.

The art of adaptation extends beyond the confines of the kitchen, permeating the menus of restaurants, the aisles of grocery stores, and the offerings of food delivery services. As consumers increasingly seek options that align with their dietary preferences, establishments respond by incorporating adapted classics into their culinary repertoire. Plant-based lasagnas, gluten-free pizzas, and keto-friendly desserts become niche offerings and mainstream choices, reflecting a culinary landscape that values inclusivity and customization.

Moreover, adapting classic recipes is not solely a matter of dietary necessity but often a conscious choice driven by a desire for a healthier lifestyle. In an era where health-consciousness is on the rise, classic recipes undergo modifications that prioritize nutrient density, whole ingredients, and mindful cooking techniques. Adding superfoods, such as quinoa, kale, or chia seeds, to traditional dishes infuses them with an extra layer of nutritional richness, catering to a demographic that seeks taste and wellness in their culinary choices.

In conclusion, adapting classic recipes for dietary preferences is a dynamic and evolving journey that harmonizes tradition with the ever-changing landscape of culinary preferences. This transformation process celebrates inclusivity, creativity, and the recognition that the joy of iconic dishes should be accessible to all. Whether driven by ethical considerations, health- conscious choices, or a desire for culinary exploration, the art of adaptation ensures that the rich tapestry of classic recipes continues to unfold, inviting individuals to savor the familiar while embracing the exciting possibilities that arise from a culinary landscape that adapts to the diverse needs and tastes of its enthusiasts.

Tips for successful gluten-free and vegan baking

Navigating the realm of gluten-free and vegan baking is a culinary adventure that requires a blend of creativity, precision, and an understanding of the unique characteristics of alternative ingredients. Whether driven by dietary preferences, health considerations, or the need to accommodate food sensitivities, the journey of gluten-free and vegan baking opens the door to a world of possibilities. Successful execution of these baking endeavors involves embracing a set of tips that not only ensure the absence of gluten and animal products but promise delightful, flavorful results that rival their traditional counterparts.

One of the foundational aspects of successful gluten-free and vegan baking lies in the selection and combination of alternative flour. Traditional wheat flour, a staple in conventional baking, provides gluten—a protein contributing to baked goods' structure and elasticity. Gluten-free flour like rice, almond, coconut, and chickpea flour step into the spotlight without wheat. The key to success lies in crafting a blend of these flours that mimics the texture and structure of traditional recipes. This combination not only addresses the absence of gluten but also introduces a spectrum of flavors and nutrients, contributing to the complexity and depth of the final product.

Moreover, adding binding agents is paramount in gluten-free and vegan baking, where the absence of eggs—commonly used as binders in traditional recipes—poses a challenge. Ingredients like flaxseed meal, chia seeds, applesauce, or mashed bananas are adequate egg substitutes, lending the necessary cohesion to batters and doughs. These alternatives mimic the binding properties of eggs and introduce unique flavors and nutritional benefits, adding depth to the overall composition of the baked goods.

In gluten-free and vegan baking, the role of leavening agents becomes crucial in achieving the desired rise and texture. Baking powder and baking soda, often used in conventional recipes, play a pivotal role in these adaptations. However, the absence of eggs necessitates additional considerations. Apple cider vinegar, when combined with baking soda, creates a reaction that mimics the leavening effect of eggs. This dynamic duo contributes to the rise of baked goods and imparts a subtle tanginess that enhances the flavor profile.

Sweeteners in gluten-free and vegan baking are another element that demands careful consideration. Traditional recipes often rely on refined sugars, but options like maple syrup, agave nectar, coconut sugar, and date sugar become go-to choices when seeking healthier alternatives. These natural sweeteners not only add sweetness but also introduce nuanced flavors that complement the other ingredients. The liquid nature of some sweeteners may necessitate adjustments to the overall moisture content in the recipe, requiring a delicate balance to achieve the desired consistency.

Including fats in gluten-free and vegan baking is integral to achieving the desired texture and mouthfeel. While butter is a common fat source in traditional recipes, vegan alternatives like coconut, avocado, or plant-based margarine provide the necessary richness. These fats contribute to the tender crumb and moistness of the final product, ensuring that the absence of dairy does not compromise the overall sensory experience.

Additionally, the role of liquids in gluten-free and vegan baking extends beyond moisture content. Dairy-free milk alternatives, such as almond milk, coconut milk, or soy milk, become essential components that add liquid and contribute to the baked goods' flavor profile. The choice of liquid can impact the overall richness and depth of the final product, allowing for a degree of customization based on individual preferences.

In gluten-free baking, the use of xanthan gum or guar gum is often recommended to enhance the texture and structure of the final product. These gums act as binders and thickeners, compensating for the absence of gluten. However, using them judiciously is essential, as an excess can lead to a gummy or overly dense texture. Careful measurement and understanding of each recipe's specific requirements are crucial to achieving the desired balance. Temperature and baking times take on heightened significance in gluten-free and vegan baking. These recipes may require slightly lower or higher temperatures than their traditional counterparts, and the baking time might need adjustment. Regular monitoring and testing for doneness—whether through the toothpick test or visual cues—are essential to ensure that the baked goods achieve the ideal texture and flavor. Overbaking can result in dryness while underbaking may lead to a gummy or raw interior.

Furthermore, patience becomes a virtue in gluten-free and vegan baking, especially when allowing baked goods to cool. Unlike traditional recipes, where the cooling process may be less critical, gluten-free and vegan treats often benefit from a more extended cooling period. This allows the structure to set, ensuring a better texture and preventing the risk of crumbling. Resisting the temptation to dive into freshly baked goods straight from the oven is a small price to pay for the reward of a perfectly textured final product.

Experimentation and adaptation are hallmarks of successful gluten-free and vegan baking. The nuances of alternative ingredients and the absence of traditional elements demand a willingness to explore, adjust, and refine recipes. Each kitchen becomes a laboratory, and each batch of cookies, muffins, or bread is an experiment in flavor and texture. Embracing the learning curve and viewing the process as a culinary adventure allow bakers to cultivate a repertoire of tried-and-true recipes tailored to their tastes and preferences.

Beyond the technical aspects, successful gluten-free and vegan baking involves celebrating alternative ingredients' vibrant flavors and textures. Rather than viewing dietary restrictions as limitations, this baking style encourages a broader exploration of diverse grains, nuts, seeds, and plant-based ingredients. Far from mere substitutes, the resulting creations become unique culinary expressions that stand on their merit, offering a rich tapestry of tastes that appeal to a broad audience, regardless of dietary preferences.

In conclusion, the art of gluten-free and vegan baking is a journey that requires a blend of science, creativity, and a willingness to embrace the inherent challenges. Adapting classic recipes to meet these dietary preferences opens up possibilities, introducing a spectrum of flavors, textures, and nutritional benefits. Success in this realm lies in a thoughtful approach to ingredient selection, an understanding of the unique properties of alternative elements, and a willingness to experiment and adapt. As bakers embark on this culinary adventure, they discover that gluten-free and vegan baking is not merely a substitution of ingredients but a celebration of the diverse and delicious possibilities that emerge when tradition meets innovation in the world of baking.

Delicious alternatives for all to enjoy

Delicious alternatives for all to enjoy represent a culinary landscape that transcends dietary restrictions, preferences, and sensitivities, inviting a diverse audience to partake in the joy of flavorful and satisfying meals. In a world where nutritional choices vary widely, from vegetarian and vegan lifestyles to gluten-free, keto, and beyond, the quest for delicious alternatives becomes a universal pursuit that harmonizes taste, nutrition, and inclusivity. These alternatives cater to the needs of individuals with specific dietary requirements and redefine what constitutes a delightful and fulfilling culinary experience.

Vegetarian and vegan alternatives, in particular, have undergone a culinary renaissance, breaking free from the stereotype of bland and uninspiring fare. Plant-based cuisine, once relegated to the margins, now graces the center stage of gastronomy, showcasing the myriad ways in which fruits, vegetables, grains, and legumes can be transformed into culinary masterpieces. For instance, the evolution of plant-based burgers has redefined the classic notion of a burger, introducing patties crafted from black beans, mushrooms, lentils, or pea protein that rival their meat counterparts in taste and texture. These alternatives provide a satisfying and flavorful option for those who eschew meat and contribute to a more sustainable and environmentally conscious approach to food.

Gluten-free alternatives, a necessity for individuals with celiac disease or gluten intolerance, have transcended the realm of mere substitutions to become culinary creations that stand on their merit. The once-limiting world of gluten-free baking has expanded to include a plethora of flours—almond, coconut, rice, quinoa—that address dietary restrictions and contribute unique flavors and textures to various baked goods. Gluten-free pasta made from rice, corn, or legumes has become a staple, offering a satisfying and indistinguishable alternative to traditional wheat-based pasta. These alternatives provide a solution for those with gluten-related health concerns and offer a delicious and inclusive option for all to enjoy.

The rise of keto-friendly alternatives speaks to a growing awareness of the impact of carbohydrates on health and wellness. The ketogenic diet, characterized by low-carbohydrate and high-fat intake, has inspired a wave of culinary creativity that extends beyond traditional restrictions. Once a humble vegetable, Cauliflower transforms into a versatile ingredient, serving as a base for pizza crusts, rice, and even mashed potatoes. Almond flour and coconut flour become staples in the kitchen, crafting delicious alternatives to traditional baked goods that cater to a low-carb lifestyle. These alternatives not only adhere to the principles of the keto diet but also offer a flavorful and satisfying option for those seeking a balance between taste and nutritional considerations.

Dairy-free alternatives, driven by concerns about lactose intolerance, ethical considerations, or a desire for healthier choices, have become integral components of modern culinary repertoire. Plant-based alternatives, such as almond milk, soy milk, coconut milk, and oat milk, provide lactose-free options and contribute nuanced flavors and textures to sweet and savory dishes. Vegan cheeses once met with skepticism, have evolved to become sophisticated alternatives crafted from nuts, seeds, and plant-based proteins, offering a rich and savory experience that rivals their dairy counterparts. These alternatives accommodate dietary preferences and contribute to a more compassionate and sustainable approach to food.

The world of delicious alternatives is not confined to dietary substitutions but extends to ethnic and cultural cuisines. Plant-based renditions of traditional dishes from various culinary traditions showcase the adaptability and creativity inherent in the culinary arts. Vegan curries, stir-fries, tacos, and sushi demonstrate that the absence of animal products does not equate to a lack of flavor or cultural authenticity. These alternatives cater to those with specific dietary preferences and contribute to the global movement toward a more inclusive and diverse culinary landscape.

Moreover, the quest for delicious alternatives extends to the realm of desserts, where indulgence and dietary considerations converge. Vegan and gluten-free desserts once considered an oxymoron, have become a thriving category of culinary delights. Decadent chocolate cakes, creamy cheesecakes, and fudgy brownies crafted without dairy or gluten showcase the ingenuity of bakers in creating alternatives that satisfy the sweet tooth without compromising on taste and texture. These alternatives cater to specific dietary needs and redefine the boundaries of what is possible in the world of sweet treats.

The popularity of delicious alternatives is further fueled by a shift in consumer preferences driven by a desire for transparency, sustainability, and a holistic approach to wellness. The demand for plant-based options in restaurants, supermarkets, and food delivery services reflects a cultural shift toward a more conscious and compassionate approach to food choices. As a result, the culinary landscape is evolving to accommodate diverse tastes and preferences, ensuring that delicious alternatives are not relegated to niche markets but become mainstream choices accessible to all.

In the pursuit of delicious alternatives, the role of innovation and culinary creativity cannot be overstated.

Chefs, home cooks, and food entrepreneurs continually push the boundaries of what is possible, experimenting with ingredients, techniques, and cultural influences to create alternatives that meet dietary needs and elevate the overall culinary experience. From jackfruit-pulled "pork" sandwiches to aquafaba-based meringues, the world of delicious options is a canvas where chefs paint with flavors, textures, and culinary traditions to craft unique and delightful offerings.

As the culinary landscape continues to evolve, the emphasis on delicious alternatives becomes not just a matter of necessity but a celebration of diversity, inclusivity, and the rich tapestry of global flavors. The recognition that delightful food can and should be enjoyed by everyone, regardless of dietary preferences or restrictions, marks a paradigm shift in how we approach and appreciate culinary experiences. In a world where the choices on our plates contribute to broader conversations about health, sustainability, and ethical considerations, delicious alternatives become a testament to the transformative power of food to unite, nourish, and delight all who gather around the table.

CHAPTER VII

Sharing the Joy

Gifting classic crinkles and sugar sparkles

Gifting classic crinkles and sugar sparkles is more than a gesture; it's a delightful expression of warmth, nostalgia, and the joy of sharing handmade treats. In a world where material gifts often come and go, presenting a carefully crafted batch of classic crinkles or sugar-sparkled cookies transcends the tangible, offering a taste of tradition and a moment of shared sweetness. The allure of gifting these iconic treats lies in their delectable flavors and the emotions and memories they evoke, making them the perfect tokens of affection for many occasions.

Classic crinkles, with their distinctive cracked exteriors and soft, fudgy centers, are more than just cookies; they are edible emblems of tradition and comfort. Gifting a box of chocolate crinkles, dusted with a snowy layer of powdered sugar, is akin to presenting a parcel of cherished memories. With their timeless appeal, these cookies become vessels that carry the warmth of family gatherings, the laughter of shared moments, and the nostalgia of holiday traditions. Gifting classic crinkles becomes a way to share a dessert and a slice of one's history, inviting the recipient to partake in the simple joys that have graced the baker's kitchen and family table for generations.

Sugar sparkles, those glistening crystals that adorn cookies and cakes with a touch of magic, elevate gifting to a form of edible artistry. A beautifully decorated batch of sugar-sparkled treats is not merely a confection but a visual delight, a testament to the care and creativity invested in its creation. Gifting sugar sparkles becomes a gesture of sharing not just a treat but a piece of edible beauty, a dazzling spectacle that brings joy to both the eyes and the palate. The sparkles, whether delicately arranged on a sugar cookie or generously sprinkled on a cake, become edible expressions of love, making the act of gifting an experience that goes beyond the taste buds.

The choice to gift classic crinkles and sugar sparkles extends beyond mere desserts; it is an intentional decision to create a moment of connection. In a fast-paced world, where communication often takes digital forms, presenting homemade treats becomes a tangible expression of thoughtfulness and care. Gifting classic crinkles and sugar sparkles is an invitation to slow down, savor the moment, and engage in the simple yet profound act of sharing joy through food. Whether exchanged between friends, family members, or colleagues, these treats become bridges that connect individuals and create shared experiences.

The versatility of classic crinkles and sugar sparkles as gifts extends to many occasions. Birthdays adorned with crinkle-topped cupcakes, holidays featuring a sparkling array of cookies, or a simple gesture of appreciation expressed through a box of homemade treats—all these moments become enriched by the presence of these iconic delights. Gifting classic crinkles and sugar sparkles becomes a way to mark celebrations, express sentiments, and create lasting memories. It is a universal language that transcends cultural and linguistic barriers, speaking directly to the heart through the universal love of good food.

Moreover, gifting classic crinkles and sugar sparkles becomes a form of personal expression and creativity. The choice of flavors, the artful presentation, and the selection of specific recipes convey a unique message tailored to the preferences and tastes of the recipient. Gifting becomes an opportunity to showcase culinary skills and an understanding of the individual's likes and dislikes. The personal touch of homemade treats adds an extra layer of significance, transforming giving into a form of self- expression beyond the commercial exchange of gifts.

In holiday gifting, classic crinkles and sugar sparkles take on a special significance. Christmas, Hanukkah, Eid, Diwali, or any festive occasion becomes an opportunity to create an assortment of treats that reflect the season's spirit. The vibrant colors, positive shapes, and the sparkle of sugar crystals evoke the magic of the holidays, turning a simple gift into a festive celebration. Gifting these treats during the holiday season becomes a tradition, a way to spread joy and indulge in the sweetness of shared moments.

Gifting classic crinkles and sugar sparkles also extends its reach to expressions of gratitude and appreciation. A box of carefully crafted treats becomes a heartfelt way to say thank you, whether for a kind gesture, a helping hand, or simply for being a presence in one's life. In a professional context, these treats become memorable tokens of appreciation, fostering positive relationships and creating a sense of camaraderie among colleagues and clients. In this context, gifting becomes a form of corporate kindness, bridging the gap between professional interactions and personal connections.

The process of gifting classic crinkles and sugar sparkles is not confined to the act of giving but extends to the anticipation and joy of receiving. The moment a beautifully wrapped box of treats is presented, there is a shared sense of excitement and curiosity. The recipient is not just accepting a gift; they are unwrapping a package of delight, embarking on a sensory journey that engages sight, smell, and taste. Receiving these treats becomes a moment of pure joy, a tangible manifestation of the thought and care invested by the giver.

Furthermore, gifting classic crinkles and sugar sparkles aligns with the current cultural shift toward handmade, artisanal, and locally sourced products. In an era where consumers seek authenticity and connection with the origins of their goods, homemade treats become a cherished alternative to mass-produced, commercial gifts. Gifting classic crinkles and sugar sparkles celebrates craftsmanship, tradition, and the personal touch that defines artisanal creations. It rejects the impersonal nature of store-bought gifts in favor of a more intimate and meaningful exchange.

The joy of gifting classic crinkles and sugar sparkles also lies in the communal experience it fosters. Whether baked individually or as part of a group effort, creating these treats becomes a shared endeavor that brings people together in the kitchen. The laughter, the camaraderie, and the collaborative spirit enhance the joy of giving, turning the act of baking into a cherished tradition. In this context, the kitchen transforms into a hub of creativity and connection, where memories are made, and the act of gifting becomes an extension of the shared experience. In conclusion, gifting classic crinkles and sugar sparkles celebrates tradition, creativity, and the joy of shared moments. With their timeless appeal, these iconic treats satisfy the palate and evoke emotions and memories that make them the perfect gifts for a myriad of occasions. Whether exchanged between friends, family members, colleagues, or as tokens of gratitude, gifting classic crinkles and sugar sparkles transcends the ordinary to create moments of connection, warmth, and shared delight. It is a gesture that speaks the language of love, expressed through the universal joy of good food.

Hosting cookie exchange parties

Hosting cookie exchange parties is more than a festive gathering; it celebrates friendship, creativity, and the joy of sharing delectable treats. The tradition of cookie exchanges has been a cherished part of holiday festivities for decades, bringing people together in a spirit of camaraderie and culinary delight. The concept is simple yet profound: each participant bakes a large batch of their favorite cookies and, in turn, enjoys an assortment of others baked. This delightful exchange fills homes with the aroma of freshly baked goods and creates a sense of community and shared joy that defines the holiday season.

The allure of hosting a cookie exchange party lies in its ability to combine the joy of baking with the pleasure of socializing. Preparing for such an event often begins with carefully selecting recipes. Participants choose their favorite cookie recipes that evoke memories of family traditions or reflect their culinary creativity. The diverse array of cookies from these recipes ensures a delightful assortment that caters to various tastes and preferences. From classic chocolate chip cookies to intricately decorated sugar cookies, each batch uniquely expresses the baker's personality and culinary prowess.

As the date of the cookie exchange approaches, the kitchen becomes a hub of activity and anticipation. Flour is sifted, butter is softened, and measuring cups clink as ingredients are carefully portioned. The rhythmic whir of mixers and the sweet scent of vanilla extract fill the air, signaling the transformation of raw ingredients into delectable treats. Baking becomes a labor of love, a creative endeavor that extends beyond making cookies to the joy of sharing a piece of one's culinary passion with others.

The day of the cookie exchange arrives, and the host's home is transformed into a festive haven of holiday cheer. The dining table, adorned with seasonal decorations and a touch of twinkling lights, becomes the event's centerpiece. Each participant arrives not just with their carefully baked cookies but with the anticipation of an afternoon filled with laughter, conversation, and indulgence in sweet delights. Bringing together friends, family, or neighbors to share the joy of homemade cookies becomes a tradition fostering a sense of belonging and community.

The actual exchange of cookies is a moment of pure delight. Plates, platters, and tins adorned with cookies line the table, creating a visual feast that captures the season's spirit. Participants swap stories about their chosen recipes, the inspiration behind their creations, and the occasional mishaps that add a touch of humor to the baking process. The exchange is not just about cookies but the stories, traditions, and memories each batch represents. It's a celebration of the unique culinary journeys that converge in a delightful array of cookies.

The beauty of a cookie exchange lies in its inclusivity. Regardless of their level of baking expertise, participants come together to share the joy of creating and savoring homemade treats. The novice baker may bring a batch of simple yet heartwarming sugar cookies, while the more experienced baker showcases intricately decorated gingerbread houses. The diversity of cookies reflects the diverse skills and tastes of the participants, creating a harmonious tapestry of flavors that ensures something for everyone. It's a celebration of the fact that there are no stringent rules or judgments in the realm of cookies—only the simple joy of sharing.

Hosting a cookie exchange party is also an opportunity to introduce new and innovative recipes. Participants may experiment with unique flavor combinations, unconventional ingredients, or international influences. The exchange becomes a forum for culinary exploration, where participants can discover and appreciate cookies that go beyond the familiar. Whether a matcha-infused shortbread or a spiced chai snickerdoodle, the cookie exchange becomes a canvas for creativity, allowing bakers to showcase their adventurous spirit and broaden the collective palate.

Beyond the cookies themselves, hosting a cookie exchange party fosters a sense of connection and community. In a world where busy schedules and digital interactions often dominate, the cookie exchange provides a tangible and meaningful way to connect with others. The shared experience of baking, exchanging, and enjoying cookies becomes a bridge that transcends generational, cultural, and social divides. The oven's warmth mirrors the warmth of shared laughter, creating a space where friendships are strengthened and new connections are formed.

The cookie exchange party is not just a one-time event; it has become a cherished tradition that unfolds year after year. As the holiday season approaches, participants eagerly anticipate the invitation to gather and exchange cookies. The event takes on a comforting rhythm, a dependable marker of the festive season. It's common for participants to start planning their cookie recipes well in advance, eager to present a batch surpassing the previous year's creations. In this sense, the cookie exchange becomes a thread that weaves through the fabric of holiday traditions, creating a sense of continuity and shared history.

Moreover, hosting a cookie exchange party is an opportunity to infuse the gathering with additional festive elements. From hot cocoa stations to seasonal music playlists, the host can enhance the ambiance to create a truly immersive holiday experience. Cookie decorating stations with colorful icings and sprinkles add an interactive and playful dimension to the event, allowing participants to express their creativity and customize their cookies. The cookie exchange becomes a tasting event and a multisensory celebration that engages sight, smell, and touch.

The popularity of cookie exchange parties extends beyond intimate gatherings to workplaces, community centers, and larger social circles. In professional settings, colleagues come together to share not just cookies but also moments of relaxation and camaraderie amid the often hectic holiday season. Exchanging cookies creates workplace bonding, fostering a positive and festive atmosphere. Community-based cookie exchanges develop a sense of neighborhood camaraderie, where residents come together to celebrate the season and strengthen the ties that bind them.

The cookie exchange party also provides an opportunity to give back to the community. Some hosts organize cookie exchanges as charity events, encouraging participants to contribute cookies and donations for a chosen cause. Sharing spreads joy beyond the immediate circle of participants, extending the festive spirit to those in need. This altruistic dimension transforms the cookie exchange into a powerful vehicle for community engagement and philanthropy.

As the cookie exchange party draws to a close, participants leave not only with an assortment of delicious cookies but also with the warmth of shared moments and the anticipation of next year's gathering. The exchange of cookies becomes a cherished memory, a sweet bookmark in the narrative of the holiday season. Participants carry home their newfound treasures, carefully arranging them on festive platters or tucking them into decorative tins. The cookies become not just treats to be enjoyed but tokens of friendship, creativity, and the shared joy of the season.

In conclusion, hosting a cookie exchange party is a time-honored tradition that captures the essence of the holiday spirit. It celebrates the simple yet profound joy of sharing homemade treats, creating connections, and building memories. The cookie exchange party is a testament to the power of baking to foster community, ignite creativity, and spread the warmth of the holiday season. It is a tradition that transcends the act of exchanging cookies to become a cherished part of the shared narrative that defines the festive season for all who come together to bake, trade, and savor the sweetness of the holidays.

Spreading the love through homemade treats

Spreading love through homemade treats is a timeless tradition that transcends cultures, generations, and individual preferences. Crafting something delicious in one's kitchen and sharing it with others is more than a culinary endeavor; it's a gesture of warmth, connection, and care. Homemade treats, whether cookies, cakes, or confections, become vessels that carry both flavors and sentiments—expressions of love, joy, and the simple pleasure of creating something special for those we cherish.

The art of spreading love through homemade treats begins in the heart of the home—the kitchen. It's a space where raw ingredients transform into delectable creations, where the alchemy of flour, sugar, and butter gives rise to food and memories. Baking, in particular, holds a unique place in this tradition. The whir of mixers, the scent of vanilla, and the oven's warmth orchestrate a symphony of sensory delights. When infused with love, baking becomes a therapeutic and creative expression, a moment of solace and joy amid the bustle of everyday life.

The choice of treats reflects the personal touch embedded in spreading love. Whether it's a batch of classic chocolate chip cookies, a decadent layered cake, or intricately decorated cupcakes, the treats become an extension of the baker's personality and sentiment. Selecting recipes often draws from family traditions, childhood memories, or a desire to create something special for a particular occasion. The thoughtfulness invested in choosing the right treat for a loved one underscores the intention behind the gesture. Each cookie or slice of cake is a tangible manifestation of the love and care the baker wishes to convey.

Spreading love through homemade treats is not confined to special occasions; it is a year-round tradition that manifests in everyday moments. A surprise batch of cookies awaiting a weary family member after a long day, a freshly baked cake shared with neighbors, or a box of confections sent to a friend "just because"—these gestures transform ordinary days into moments of sweetness and connection. The simplicity of the act elevates it beyond a mere exchange of food; it becomes a language of love, a non-verbal expression that communicates care, appreciation, and a desire to bring joy to those around us.

Homemade treats as a vehicle for spreading love hold a universal appeal. Regardless of cultural background or personal taste preferences, receiving something crafted with care resonates on a profoundly human level. In a world that often rushes, where digital interactions can overshadow genuine connections, homemade treats provide a tangible and heartfelt way to bridge the gap. The recipient of such treats is not just enjoying a delicious morsel; they are receiving a concrete manifestation of the giver's time, effort, and affection.

Furthermore, spreading love through homemade treats extends beyond the immediate circle of family and friends. It becomes a means of fostering community, both locally and globally. Bake sales, charity events, and community gatherings centered around homemade treats unite people for a common cause. Sharing a slice of cake or a bag of cookies becomes a powerful tool for building connections, fostering a sense of belonging, and contributing to the well-being of others. In this context, homemade treats become ambassadors of kindness, breaking down barriers and creating bonds that transcend individual differences.

Spreading love through homemade treats takes on a special significance during celebratory occasions. Birthdays, holidays, weddings, and milestones become opportunities to indulge in delicious confections and create lasting memories. A birthday cake made with love, a plate of festive cookies exchanged during the holidays, or a wedding cake adorned with intricate details—all these treats become integral parts of the collective narrative that defines the joyous moments in our lives. They serve as edible symbols of love, unity, and the shared experiences that bind us.

Moreover, spreading love through homemade treats taps into the nostalgia of simpler times. It harks back to an era when kitchens were the heart of the home, and recipes were passed down through generations. Grandmothers baking cookies with grandchildren, mothers teaching daughters the secrets of a family cake recipe—these scenes paint a picture of a tradition deeply embedded in the fabric of family life. Sharing homemade treats becomes a continuation of these time-honored practices, a way of preserving and passing on the legacy of love and culinary traditions.

Spreading love through homemade treats also aligns with the growing movement toward mindful and intentional living. As consumers become more conscious of their food's ingredients and their choices' environmental impact, homemade treats offer a wholesome and sustainable alternative. The baker has control over the quality of ingredients, the sourcing of products, and the reduction of unnecessary additives. This conscious approach enhances the nutritional value of the treats and aligns with the broader movement toward mindful consumption and a return to more straightforward, more meaningful practices.

The tradition of spreading love through homemade treats is not immune to the influence of social media. In the age of Instagram and Pinterest, the presentation of treats has become an art form, with bakers sharing their creations with a global audience. This digital landscape has transformed the act of spreading love into a visual experience, with carefully curated images of beautifully plated desserts becoming a form of online expression. The virtual sharing of recipes, techniques, and inspirations has created a global community of bakers who connect and inspire one another, fostering a sense of camaraderie that transcends geographical boundaries.

In conclusion, spreading love through homemade treats is a tradition that encapsulates the essence of human connection, creativity, and the joy of giving. Whether a simple batch of cookies or an intricately crafted cake, sharing homemade treats becomes a tangible expression of love, care, and thoughtfulness. It is a tradition that resonates across cultures, generations, and modern lifestyles, providing a timeless and meaningful way to connect with others. As long as there are kitchens filled with the aroma of freshly baked goods and hearts eager to share, spreading love through homemade treats will continue to enrich our lives and create moments of sweetness in the world.

CHAPTER VIII

Modern Twists on Classics

Fusion recipes combining classic and modern flavors

Fusion recipes, marrying classic and modern flavors, herald a culinary evolution that transcends traditional boundaries and tantalizes taste buds with unexpected delights; in the dynamic landscape of gastronomy, where innovation and creativity reign supreme, fusion cuisine emerges as a captivating journey that pays homage to culinary heritage while embracing contemporary palates. The seamless blend of classic and modern flavors creates a symphony of tastes, inviting food enthusiasts on an exciting adventure that defies culinary norms and expands the realm of possibilities in the kitchen.

At the heart of fusion recipes lies a celebration of diversity and a fusion of culinary traditions. Drawing inspiration from various cultures and cuisines, chefs and home cooks embark on a flavorful exploration to harmonize contrasting elements. Classic flavors, rooted in time-honored recipes passed down through generations, meet modern twists, introducing innovative ingredients, techniques, and presentations. The result is a culinary alchemy that sparks new dimensions of taste and texture, transforming the familiar into something extraordinary.

In the realm of fusion, classic and modern flavors merge to create a culinary language that speaks to a global audience. Take, for instance, the fusion of traditional Italian pasta with Japanese flavors, giving rise to dishes like miso-infused carbonara or umami-rich soy-based bolognese. These creations pay homage to the comforting familiarity of Italian classics while infusing them with the bold and savory notes of Japanese culinary artistry. The fusion of flavors becomes a bridge that connects disparate culinary worlds, demonstrating the universality of taste and the boundless potential for creative experimentation.

Classic dishes from various regions serve as the canvas upon which modern flavors are painted, transforming the ordinary into the extraordinary. Consider the fusion of Mexican and Indian cuisines, where the iconic flavors of tacos meet the vibrant spices of curry, resulting in dishes like masala chicken tacos or biryani-inspired burritos. This fusion is a testament to the imaginative reinterpretation of culinary traditions, showcasing the adaptability and creativity inherent in the fusion movement. The melding of classic and modern flavors in these recipes sparks intrigue and reflects a broader cultural exchange, where culinary borders blur, and a new, shared culinary language emerges.

Moreover, the fusion of classic and modern flavors introduces an element of surprise that elevates the dining experience. It challenges preconceived notions and invites diners to embrace the unexpected. Picture the fusion of French pastries with Asian influences, yielding creations like matcha-infused croissants or yuzu macaron towers. In these instances, the fusion transcends the blending of ingredients to become a sensory adventure that delights the palate and stimulates the senses. The juxtaposition of classic French techniques with modern Asian flavors creates a harmonious dance of taste, texture, and visual appeal, offering a fresh perspective on beloved culinary traditions.

The innovation inherent in fusion recipes extends beyond combining ingredients to encompass cooking methods, presentation, and even cultural narratives. Classic dishes are reimagined through a modern lens, introducing techniques like molecular gastronomy, sous-vide cooking, or edible flowers for artistic flair. Consider the fusion of traditional Spanish paella with avant-garde techniques, where the socarrat meets the whimsy of foamed saffron air. This blend of classic and modern transforms the dish into a visual spectacle. It underscores the limitless possibilities when culinary traditions are approached with an open mind and a spirit of innovation.

Furthermore, fusion recipes challenge the notion of authenticity, inviting a reevaluation of culinary norms. The rigidity of adhering strictly to traditional recipes gives way to a more fluid and dynamic approach, where the essence of a dish remains intact while embracing the evolving tastes of contemporary palates. Classic Italian tiramisu, for example, may find itself infused with the bold richness of Vietnamese coffee or the smokiness of Japanese hojicha, offering a delightful twist that respects the origins of the dessert while pushing the boundaries of flavor exploration.

Cultural exchange becomes an integral part of the culinary narrative in the fusion of classic and modern flavors. The cross-pollination of ingredients and techniques from different regions fosters a global interconnectedness, where the kitchen becomes a meeting point for diverse culinary traditions. Consider the fusion of Middle Eastern and South American cuisines, where the aromatic spices of the Levant find common ground with the zesty flavors of Latin America. Dishes like sumac-infused ceviche or tahini-drizzled empanadas exemplify the fusion of cultural elements, creating a tapestry of tastes that reflects our interconnected world.

The fusion movement is not confined to restaurant kitchens but permeates home cooking, where adventurous cooks experiment with flavors and techniques to create personalized fusions. Classic family recipes handed down through generations become canvases for culinary exploration, with home cooks infusing them with modern twists inspired by their diverse culinary influences. The fusion of classic and contemporary flavors in home kitchens reflects the democratization of culinary creativity, inviting everyone to participate in the joy of reinterpreting tradition and crafting unique, personalized dishes.

However, with the innovation and excitement of fusion recipes comes the responsibility to approach the process with cultural sensitivity and respect. While fusion celebrates diversity, it is essential to avoid appropriation and ensure that the blending of culinary traditions is done in a way that acknowledges and honors the origins of the dishes. This mindful approach fosters an adventurous and respectful culinary landscape, recognizing the rich tapestry of global food culture.

In conclusion, fusion recipes that combine classic and modern flavors represent a culinary journey that transcends borders, celebrates diversity, and pushes the boundaries of gastronomic exploration. The fusion movement is a testament to the adaptability and creativity inherent in the culinary arts, showcasing the infinite possibilities when traditional and contemporary elements come together. Whether in restaurant kitchens or home settings, fusion recipes invite us to embark on a flavorful adventure that redefines culinary norms, sparks joyous surprises, and fosters a sense of global interconnectedness through the universal language of taste.

Trendy ingredients and techniques for a contemporary twist

In the dynamic world of contemporary cuisine, the infusion of trendy ingredients and innovative techniques is the driving force behind a culinary revolution. Chefs and home cooks alike are constantly seeking new ways to elevate dishes, redefine flavors, and captivate the ever- evolving palate of the modern consumer. Incorporating trendy ingredients and techniques transforms familiar recipes into culinary adventures and reflects the broader societal trends shaping how we approach food, health, and sustainability.

One of the defining features of contemporary cuisine is the exploration of novel ingredients that add depth, complexity, and uniqueness to dishes. Superfoods like quinoa, acai, and chia seeds have become staples, celebrated for their nutritional value and versatility in the kitchen. Once considered exotic, these ingredients are now readily available, allowing cooks to experiment with textures and flavors that bring a contemporary twist to traditional recipes. Consider, for example, the ubiquitous avocado toast that has become a symbol of modern gastronomy—a simple yet sophisticated marriage of creamy avocado and crusty bread, elevated with the crunch of chia seeds and a sprinkle of flaky sea salt.

Beyond superfoods, the contemporary kitchen embraces diverse ingredients that tantalize taste buds and challenge culinary norms. Fermented foods, such as kimchi and kombucha, have surged in popularity, bringing a burst of umami and complex flavors. Once confined to sushi rolls, seaweed is now celebrated for its nutritional richness and has found its way into salads, snacks, and even desserts. The fusion of global flavors, facilitated by increased accessibility to international ingredients, has given rise to innovative combinations that defy traditional culinary categorizations, such as miso-infused tacos or harissa-spiced pasta.

Innovative cooking techniques with trendy ingredients have become a hallmark of contemporary cuisine. Once reserved for avant-garde restaurants, molecular gastronomy has trickled down to home kitchens, inspiring a generation of cooks to experiment with spherification, foaming, and gelification. Sous-vide cooking, a method that involves slow-cooking vacuum-sealed ingredients in a water bath, has revolutionized how proteins are prepared, resulting in unparalleled tenderness and precision. Once relegated to outdoor grills, smoking has found its way into indoor kitchens, infusing dishes with a distinct smokiness that adds depth and complexity.

The integration of trendy ingredients and techniques is not merely a quest for novelty; it is deeply intertwined with broader societal trends and shifts in consumer preferences. For instance, the emphasis on health and wellness has propelled ingredients like turmeric, matcha, and adaptogens into the spotlight. These ingredients are celebrated for their vibrant colors, unique flavors, and purported health benefits. Smoothie bowls adorned with edible flowers, matcha lattes, and golden milk have become visual representations of the marriage between aesthetic appeal and nutritional consciousness, embodying the contemporary ethos of mindful eating.

Moreover, plant-based eating has spurred a creative reimagining of classic dishes, replacing traditional animal products with innovative plant-derived alternatives. Almond milk, coconut yogurt, and plant-based meat substitutes have become staples in kitchens catering to a growing population of flexitarians, vegetarians, and vegans. The contemporary cook seeks to create dishes that are delicious and align with ethical and environmental considerations, reflecting a conscientious approach to food choices.

The use of trendy ingredients and techniques is also closely linked to sustainability. As awareness of environmental issues grows, chefs and home cooks are exploring ways to minimize food waste, embrace local and seasonal produce, and utilize unconventional parts of ingredients that were once discarded. Root-to-stem cooking, for example, encourages the use of vegetable parts that are typically discarded, transforming kitchen scraps into flavorful additions to dishes. This sustainability-driven approach extends beyond the plate to include eco-friendly practices such as composting, sourcing ingredients locally, and reducing reliance on single-use plastics.

In the realm of desserts, contemporary pastry chefs have embraced a departure from traditional sweetness in favor of alternative sweeteners and reduced sugar content. Ingredients like coconut sugar, maple syrup, and agave nectar offer nuanced sweetness with a lower glycemic impact. Desserts featuring unconventional pairings, such as olive oil cakes with citrus and rosemary or balsamic-infused berries, showcase a departure from saccharine indulgence toward a more sophisticated and nuanced flavor profile.

The intersection of trendy ingredients and techniques is not limited to restaurant kitchens. Still, it has permeated home cooking, where passionate cooks experiment with flavors and methods to create restaurant-worthy dishes. Armed with abundant online resources and culinary inspiration, home cooks are increasingly adventurous in exploring global ingredients and cutting-edge techniques. Social media platforms serve as virtual kitchens where individuals share their culinary creations, fostering a sense of community and encouraging others to embark on their culinary journeys.

While integrating trendy ingredients and techniques enriches the contemporary culinary landscape, navigating this terrain with a balanced approach is essential. Pursuing innovation should include the importance of flavor, tradition, and cultural authenticity. The most successful contemporary dishes strike a harmonious balance between the avant-garde and the timeless, paying homage to culinary heritage while pushing the boundaries of what is possible in the kitchen.

In conclusion, infusing trendy ingredients and techniques into contemporary cuisine is a dynamic and ever-evolving exploration of flavors, textures, and culinary possibilities.

From superfoods and global flavors to innovative cooking methods, the modern kitchen is a melting pot of creativity that reflects broader societal trends and changing consumer preferences. As chefs and home cooks continue to push the boundaries of culinary expression, the fusion of classic and modern elements promises a gastronomic future that is both exciting and deliciously unpredictable.

Embracing innovation while preserving tradition

Embracing innovation while preserving tradition represents a delicate and dynamic dance within the culinary world, where chefs and home cooks navigate the intersection of creativity and heritage. In the ever- evolving landscape of gastronomy, the push for innovation is met with a profound respect for the timeless recipes and culinary legacies that form the foundation of diverse cuisines. This delicate balance seeks to transcend the confines of tradition without disregarding its essence, fostering a culinary environment where the past and present merge to create a vibrant tapestry of flavors, techniques, and experiences.

Innovation in the culinary realm manifests in various forms, from avant-garde cooking techniques to the integration of novel ingredients that challenge conventional palates. The desire to push culinary boundaries often stems from a quest for new sensory experiences, a fascination with cutting-edge technology, or a response to evolving dietary preferences and cultural shifts. Molecular gastronomy, for example, introduces scientific principles into the kitchen, transforming familiar ingredients into unexpected textures and presentations. Techniques such as spherification, foaming, and liquid nitrogen freezing exemplify the marriage of science and culinary artistry, giving rise to dishes that defy traditional expectations.

The incorporation of novel ingredients further amplifies the innovative spirit in modern kitchens. Chefs experiment with exotic fruits, heirloom grains, foraged herbs, and globally inspired spices, infusing dishes with unexpected and exciting flavors. The introduction of international ingredients broadens the culinary repertoire and reflects a globalized approach to cooking, where the world becomes a pantry rich with inspiration. However, as chefs embrace innovation, they grapple with the challenge of integrating these novel elements in a way that respects and enhances the essence of traditional dishes.

On the other hand, preserving tradition is a commitment to safeguarding culinary heritage, honoring the wisdom of generations past, and maintaining a connection to cultural roots. Traditional recipes, often passed down through families or artistic lineages, carry stories, memories, and a sense of identity. Preserving tradition in the kitchen involves more than replicating age-old recipes; it requires understanding the cultural context, regional nuances, and the significance of each ingredient. Traditional cooking methods, spice blends, and time-honored techniques form the bedrock of culinary legacies that withstand the test of time.

The delicate balance between innovation and tradition is evident in reinterpreting classic dishes. Renowned chefs worldwide embark on journeys to reimagine traditional recipes, infusing them with a contemporary flair that captivates modern palates. For instance, a classic French coq au vin might undergo a transformation with the infusion of Asian spices or the incorporation of molecular gastronomy techniques, resulting in a dish that pays homage to its roots while embracing the excitement of the new. The reinterpretation of classics is a testament to the malleability of tradition, highlighting its ability to evolve and adapt without losing its fundamental character.

Innovation and tradition coexist not only in high-end restaurant kitchens but also in the realm of everyday home cooking. Inspired by culinary trends and global flavors, home cooks often experiment with new ingredients and techniques to breathe fresh life into family recipes. Whether it's a twist on a traditional holiday dish or incorporating a trendy ingredient into a beloved recipe, home cooks play a vital role in the ongoing narrative of culinary evolution. The home kitchen becomes a canvas where innovation and tradition intersect, fostering a sense of culinary exploration within the context of cherished family rituals.

Preserving tradition in the face of innovation is a nuanced undertaking that requires a thoughtful and respectful approach. Chefs and home cooks balance the desire for creative expression with the responsibility to honor the cultural roots of their dishes. This delicate dance involves a deep understanding of the historical context, the significance of each ingredient, and the rituals associated with traditional dishes. When guided by a genuine appreciation for tradition, innovation becomes a tool for enriching rather than erasing culinary heritage.

Culinary innovation also intersects with the growing emphasis on sustainability and ethical sourcing. As chefs and home cooks explore novel ingredients, there is an increasing awareness of their choices' environmental and ethical implications. The farm-to-table movement, for example, emphasizes the importance of locally sourced, seasonal ingredients, aligning with traditional agricultural practices that have sustained communities for generations. Integrating sustainable and ethical considerations into culinary innovation reflects a broader commitment to responsible and mindful cooking that respects the past and the future.

Moreover, the evolution of culinary education mirrors the dynamic relationship between innovation and tradition.

Culinary schools, once focused on imparting classic techniques and recipes, now incorporate modules on cutting-edge technologies, global ingredients, and avant-garde methods. Aspiring chefs are encouraged to experiment with creativity while mastering traditional cooking fundamentals. This approach acknowledges that a strong foundation in tradition provides the necessary scaffolding for culinary exploration and innovation.

In multicultural societies, the intertwining of innovation and tradition celebrates diversity and cultural exchange. Culinary fusion exemplifies this harmonious blend, where different traditions converge to create something new and exciting. For instance, the fusion of Asian and Latin American flavors gives rise to dishes like Korean barbecue tacos or sushi burritos. In these creations, the culinary landscape becomes a melting pot that transcends cultural boundaries, fostering an appreciation for the richness of global gastronomy.

However, the delicate balance between innovation and tradition can be challenging. The rapid pace of culinary trends, fueled by social media and the quest for novelty, sometimes overshadow the importance of tradition. Chefs may constantly grapple with the pressure to innovate, risking the dilution or misrepresentation of traditional dishes in pursuit of the next big culinary sensation. It becomes imperative to approach innovation with a discerning eye, ensuring that it complements rather than eclipses traditional recipes' cultural authenticity and historical significance.

In conclusion, the symbiotic relationship between innovation and tradition defines the dynamic landscape of contemporary cuisine. Chefs and home cooks navigate this delicate balance, drawing inspiration from the past while embracing future possibilities. The dialogue between tradition and innovation creates a culinary environment rooted in history and open to evolution. As the gastronomic world continues to evolve, this delicate dance between the timeless and the cutting-edge promises a rich and flavorful journey that honors the essence of culinary heritage while inviting the excitement of the unknown.

CHAPTER IX

Creating Your Signature Cookie

Developing your own unique crinkle or sparkle recipe

Crafting your unique crinkle or sparkle cookie recipe is a delightful journey that allows you to infuse personal creativity into the timeless art of baking. As you embark on this culinary adventure, you step into the role of artist and alchemist, experimenting with flavors, textures, and techniques to create a signature treat that reflects your taste and style. The process begins with a foundational understanding of the classic crinkle and sparkle recipes, which have stood the test of time and captured the hearts of cookie enthusiasts across generations.

Start by immersing yourself in the world of classic crinkles and sugar sparkles, exploring the rich tapestry of ingredients and methods that define these timeless favorites. Understand the alchemy of butter, flour, sugar, and leavening agents that give crinkles characteristic texture and flavor. Delve into the magic of sugar sparkles, where the simplicity of sugar is transformed into an artful coating that adds a satisfying crunch and visual appeal to each bite. Familiarize yourself with the variations within the classic recipes, from chocolate-infused crinkles to the subtle sweetness of vanilla sugar sparkles.

With this foundation in place, it's time to let your imagination take the lead. Consider the flavor profile you wish to impart to your crinkles or sparkles — perhaps a hint of citrus zest for freshness, a dash of spice for warmth, or the richness of nuts for added texture. Experiment with different types of sugars, exploring the nuanced sweetness of brown sugar or the molasses undertones of muscovado. Allow your creativity to guide your choice of extracts, from the floral notes of almond to the warmth of vanilla, infusing your creation with a distinctive aroma.

The texture is pivotal in the allure of crinkles and sparkles, so explore a spectrum of add-ins to elevate your recipe. Chopped nuts, dried fruits, or even a decadent swirl of chocolate can introduce layers of complexity and surprise. Embrace the tactile experience of baking, experimenting with ingredient ratios to achieve the perfect balance between softness and chewiness in your crinkles or the ideal crispness in your sugar sparkles.

As you venture into the realm of unique flavors and textures, take notice of the visual appeal of your creations. The allure of crinkles lies in their crackled appearance, a visual symphony of contrasting textures that beckons with the promise of a soft interior. Similarly, sugar sparkles captivate with their glistening coating, inviting a sensory experience that begins with the eyes and extends to the palate. Consider incorporating natural dyes or decorative elements to add a touch of whimsy and make your crinkles or sparkles a treat for the taste buds and a feast for the eyes.

Precision and patience are your allies in the quest for the perfect crinkle or sparkle. Baking is an exact science, and minor ingredient quantities or oven temperature adjustments can yield vastly different results. Take the time to measure each ingredient carefully, noting the impact of subtle changes on the final product. Allow your dough to chill adequately for crinkles that hold their shape and develop the trademark cracks upon baking. Pay attention to the consistency of your sugar sparkle mixture to achieve a coating that strikes the ideal balance between sweetness and crunch.

The beauty of creating your crinkle or sparkle recipe lies in the iterative refinement process. Don't be discouraged by the occasional misstep; view each batch as an opportunity to learn and adjust. Keep a record of your experiments, noting the variations in ingredients, proportions, and baking times. This culinary journal becomes a treasure trove of insights, allowing you to hone in on the unique combination that captures your vision for the perfect crinkle or sparkle.

Sharing your creations with friends, family, or baking enthusiasts adds more joy. Invite others to taste and provide feedback on your evolving recipes. The communal aspect of baking fosters a sense of connection and shared delight, turning your kitchen into a hub of creativity and enjoyment. Whether you present your crinkles and sparkles in beautifully crafted gift boxes or share them at gatherings, sharing transforms your creations into a gesture of love and camaraderie.

In pursuing your own unique crinkle or sparkle recipe, embrace the spirit of experimentation and discovery. Allow the kitchen to become your laboratory, where you test hypotheses and unlock the secrets to your ideal cookie. Celebrate the fusion of tradition and innovation as you draw inspiration from classic recipes while fearlessly charting your course. Remember that the essence of baking lies not only in the final product but in the joyous journey of creation itself. With patience, passion, and a dash of imagination, you'll unveil a crinkle or sparkle recipe that carries the mark of your culinary identity — a delicious testament to your artistry in baking.

Tips for experimenting with flavors and textures

Embarking on the thrilling adventure of experimenting with flavors and textures in the culinary realm opens up a world of creative possibilities, transforming cooking into an art form that engages the senses and entices the palate. Whether you're a seasoned chef or an enthusiastic home cook, the journey of flavor and texture experimentation is a dynamic exploration that adds depth, nuance, and excitement to your culinary repertoire. At the heart of this endeavor lies the understanding that flavors and textures are the building blocks of a memorable dining experience, and mastering the art of their interplay allows you to craft dishes that transcend the ordinary and delight the senses.

Begin your experimentation by developing a keen palate and a mindful approach to tasting. Cultivate an appreciation for the nuances of individual ingredients, recognizing the spectrum of flavors they contribute to a dish. Consider the interplay between sweetness, acidity, bitterness, saltiness, and umami, allowing your taste buds to discern the subtlest notes. This heightened sensory awareness is the foundation for crafting harmonious flavor profiles and layering textures that complement one another.

Exploration of flavors involves a willingness to think beyond the familiar and embrace the unexpected. Experiment with contrasting tastes, pairing sweet and savory elements to create a symphony of flavors on the palate. To add complexity and depth, consider infusing dishes with incredible herbs, spices, or aromatic ingredients. The fusion of global flavors provides a vast playground for experimentation, allowing you to draw inspiration from diverse culinary traditions and bring a worldly flair to your creations.

Texture experimentation is an art that invites you to play with contrasts that captivate the senses. Consider the interplay between crisp, tender, smooth, crunchy, and velvety and granular. Texture adds a dynamic dimension to each bite, elevating the dining experience beyond taste alone. Experiment with various cooking techniques to achieve the desired textures, from grilling and roasting to braising and sous-vide cooking. Mastering texture involves a balance that complements the overall composition of a dish, enhancing its visual appeal and mouthfeel.

Seasoning emerges as a critical element in the art of flavor experimentation. Elevate your dishes by exploring various salts, spices, and herbs. Experiment with infused oils, flavored vinegar, and unique condiments to impart distinctive notes to your creations. The judicious use of seasonings allows you to highlight specific flavors, enhance the overall taste profile, and surprise the palate with unexpected twists. As you experiment with herbs, be mindful of their potency and their impact on the final dish.

Consider the art of layering flavors, creating depth through the thoughtful integration of multiple taste sensations. Start with a base flavor and build complexity by adding complementary or contrasting elements. For example, a citrusy marinade might complement a rich and savory glaze, creating a multidimensional taste experience. The layering of flavors allows you to orchestrate a culinary symphony that unfolds with each bite, revealing a progression of tastes that linger on the palate.

Texture experimentation extends to the realm of baking, where the interplay of ingredients and techniques defines the character of your creations. Play with the ratios of fats, sugars, and leavening agents to achieve the desired texture in cookies, cakes, and pastries. Experiment with alternative flours like almond or coconut to add depth and nuttiness to your baked goods. Incorporating mix-ins, such as nuts, chocolate, or fruit, introduces layers of texture that elevate your baked treats to new heights.

As you delve into flavor and texture experimentation, remember the importance of balance. The art lies in creating a harmonious blend where no single element dominates, allowing each flavor and texture to contribute to the overall symphony of the dish. Be attentive to your ingredients' subtleties and interactions, adjusting proportions and combinations until you achieve a cohesive and well-rounded result. This pursuit of balance ensures that your culinary creations are exciting and consistently enjoyable.

Experimenting with flavors and textures is inherently dynamic, requiring a willingness to iterate and refine your creations. Treat each experiment as a learning opportunity, embracing successes and setbacks as valuable steps in your culinary journey. Maintain a sense of curiosity and playfulness in the kitchen, allowing your creativity to flourish without the constraints of rigid recipes. The freedom to improvise and adapt is at the core of flavor and texture experimentation, fostering a sense of ownership and authenticity in your culinary endeavors.

A crucial aspect of successful experimentation is the art of pairing, where flavors and textures complement and enhance one another. Consider the synergy between ingredients, explore classic pairings, and dare to discover unexpected combinations. Wine and food pairings provide a rich source of inspiration, as the nuanced flavors of different varietals can guide your choices in the kitchen. Experiment with the interplay of sweet and savory, crisp and creamy, light and bold, recognizing that the right pairing can elevate the dining experience to a sublime level.

Technology and modern culinary tools offer additional avenues for flavor and texture experimentation exploration. Techniques such as molecular gastronomy, sous-vide cooking, and foaming allow you to push the boundaries of traditional cooking, creating innovative textures and presentations. While these methods may require additional skill and precision, they open doors to culinary possibilities that challenge conventional norms and spark the imagination.

In conclusion, experimenting with flavors and textures is a dynamic and enriching journey that transforms cooking into a creative expression of personal style and taste. Whether crafting savory dishes, baking delectable treats, or exploring the world of molecular gastronomy, the key lies in mindfulness, curiosity, and a willingness to push boundaries. Embrace the joy of discovery in the kitchen, and let your culinary experiments reflect the unique essence of your culinary identity. As you navigate the intricate dance of flavors and textures, savor the excitement of creating dishes that nourish the body and delight the senses in a symphony of taste and texture.

Sharing your creations with friends and family

Sharing your culinary creations with friends and family is a heartwarming tradition that transcends the act of cooking, transforming it into a meaningful and communal experience. The essence of this sharing extends far beyond the mere exchange of dishes; it embodies the spirit of connection, love, and joy that comes from nourishing both the body and the soul. As you present your carefully crafted dishes to those close to you, you become a cook and storyteller, weaving narratives of tradition, creativity, and shared moments around the dining table.

Sharing food is deeply rooted in cultural and familial traditions, transcending geographical boundaries and bridging generations. It is a universal language communicating care, hospitality, and a desire to create lasting memories. Whether passing down cherished family recipes or introducing loved ones to your latest culinary experiments, sharing becomes a tangible expression of love and a celebration of togetherness.

In the context of familial bonds, sharing homemade meals is a time-honored ritual that fosters a sense of connection and continuity. Passed down through generations, family recipes carry the flavors of the past and the stories and traditions that define a family's unique identity. Sharing becomes a way to honor these culinary legacies, ensuring that the essence of family traditions lives on through the sizzle of pans and the aroma of familiar spices.

Friendship, too, finds a special place at the shared table. When you share your culinary creations with friends, you extend an invitation into your world, offering them a taste of your culinary identity. The shared meal symbolizes camaraderie, breaking down barriers and creating a space for laughter, conversation, and the forging of lasting bonds. Whether hosting elaborate dinner parties or simply gathering for a casual brunch, sharing transforms the ordinary into the extraordinary, fostering a sense of community and appreciation.

Sharing homemade dishes is a manifestation of generosity and a gesture of love that transcends words. Preparing and sharing a meal becomes a tangible expression of care and thoughtfulness in a world often characterized by fast-paced living, busy schedules, and digital interactions. It is a pause in the rhythm of life, an opportunity to connect on a deeper level, and a reminder that, amid our hectic lives, there is value in slowing down to savor the simple pleasures of shared meals.

Furthermore, sharing invites a sense of vulnerability and authenticity into the culinary experience. When you present your creations to others, you are offering a plate of food and a piece of yourself. Your choice of ingredients, flavors, and presentation reflects your taste, style, and the care you invest in each dish. Sharing becomes an act of self-expression, an opportunity to showcase your creativity and to invite others into your culinary world.

The shared table is a space for storytelling, where each dish carries a narrative that transcends its physical form. It becomes a canvas on which you paint tales of culinary inspiration, cultural exploration, and personal growth. As friends and family gather around, the stories behind each dish unfold, creating a rich tapestry of experiences that go beyond the flavors on the plate. The act of sharing becomes a dynamic dialogue that spans cultures, memories, and the shared joy of discovery.

Moreover, sharing your creations becomes a way to celebrate milestones, achievements, and moments of joy. Birthdays, anniversaries, graduations, and other special occasions resonate in the shared meal, where the collective enjoyment of good food becomes a focal point of celebration. The shared table becomes a space for raising toasts, expressing gratitude, and creating cherished memories that linger in the hearts of those gathered.

The shared culinary experience extends beyond the home kitchen and dining table confines. Potluck gatherings, community events, and food festivals become platforms for spreading the joy of sharing to a broader audience. Contributing a dish to a communal feast is a way of participating in a collective culinary narrative where diverse flavors and traditions converge. It is an opportunity to showcase your culinary skills, exchange ideas, and revel in the joy of discovering new tastes alongside fellow enthusiasts.

In the digital age, sharing culinary creations takes on new dimensions through social media platforms. Food blogs, Instagram accounts, and online communities become virtual spaces where home cooks and professional chefs share their culinary journeys with a global audience. The act of sharing transcends geographical boundaries, allowing individuals to connect, inspire, and be inspired by the diverse array of culinary experiences from around the world. The virtual table becomes a platform for fostering a global culinary conversation where sharing extends beyond the immediate circle of friends and family.

The act of sharing your creations has its challenges. Whether simple or elaborate, culinary endeavors require time, effort, and a degree of vulnerability. The fear of judgment or criticism may linger, especially when presenting creations that deviate from traditional norms. However, it is in overcoming these challenges that the act of sharing becomes even more meaningful. Embracing the imperfections, learning from experiences, and remaining open to feedback contribute to the evolution of your culinary skills and deepen the authenticity of the shared experience.

In conclusion, sharing your culinary creations with friends and family is a multifaceted and profoundly enriching endeavor. It is an expression of love, a celebration of tradition, and a bridge that connects individuals across cultures and generations. As you present your carefully crafted dishes to those around you, you are not merely sharing a meal; you create moments of joy, build lasting memories, and invite others to join you in a culinary journey that transcends time and space. The shared table becomes a space where stories are told, connections are forged, and sharing transforms the ordinary into the extraordinary.

CHAPTER X

Cookie Adventures Around the World

Exploring International Cookie Traditions

Exploring international cookie traditions unveils a fascinating tapestry of flavors, techniques, and cultural nuances passed down through generations, shaping how people around the world indulge in sweet delights. Cookies, known by various names and forms, serve as ambassadors of culinary heritage, carrying the unique essence of each culture and reflecting the diverse ways communities express love, celebrate festivities, and share moments of joy.

In France's heart, the delicate buttery sablé cookies capture the essence of French patisserie. These shortbread wonders, often infused with the floral notes of lavender or the citrusy zest of lemon, crumble delicately on the tongue. Their simplicity belies a rich history that dates back to the medieval town of Sablé-sur-Sarthe, where buttery biscuits were first created. Today, sablés are enjoyed in countless variations across France, each region adding its twist to this classic cookie, whether it's a sprinkling of almonds in Provence or a touch of sea salt in Brittany.

The Italian Santucci, also known as biscotti, offers a crunchy and twice-baked delight that symbolizes Italian coffee culture. Originating in Prato in Tuscany, Santucci was historically favored by sailors for their long shelf life. During celebrations, these oblong cookies are packed with almonds and anise seeds, traditionally dipped in Vin Santo, a sweet dessert wine. The ritual of dunking Santucci into wine or coffee transcends generations, embodying the conviviality and communal spirit of Italian gatherings.

Journeying to the heart of Scandinavia, the Swedish pepparkakor introduces a spicy and aromatic experience reminiscent of the festive season. Traditionally enjoyed during Christmas, these gingerbread cookies are infused with cinnamon, ginger, and cloves. Often intricately shaped with festive motifs, pepparkakor not only tantalizes the taste buds but also serves as a decorative element adorning Swedish households during the holiday season. The aroma of these spiced wonders wafting through the air is synonymous with the warmth and coziness of Swedish winters.

In South America, alfajores, particularly popular in Argentina, showcase the rich tapestry of cookie traditions influenced by Spanish and indigenous flavors. These delicate sandwich cookies consist of two buttery rounds filled with dulce de leche, creating a perfect balance of sweetness and richness. Alfajores embody the cultural fusion that characterizes South American cuisine, marrying European techniques with the sweetness of local ingredients. Whether enjoyed with a cup of mate or as a dessert centerpiece during celebrations, alfajores hold a special place in the hearts of those who appreciate the artistry of South American baking.

The Levant region introduces ma'amoul, delicate-filled cookies that are a cherished part of Middle Eastern festivities, especially during religious holidays such as Eid—crafted with semolina, flour, and butter, ma'amoul envelopes various fillings, from dates and figs to nuts and sweetened coconut. The intricate designs pressed onto the cookies using wooden molds or specialized tongs add an artistic touch, making ma'amoul a treat for the palate and a feast for the eyes. These cookies exemplify the meticulous craftsmanship and dedication to tradition that define Middle Eastern baking.

Venturing to the heart of Asia, China presents almond cookies, a delightful fusion of sweet and nutty flavors. These golden-hued treats, often adorned with a single almond in the center, have become symbolic offerings during Chinese New Year celebrations. The almond's auspicious connotations of good luck and longevity make these cookies a staple on festive tables. With a crumbly texture and the subtle aroma of almond extract, these cookies represent the intersection of culinary symbolism and delicious indulgence in Chinese culture.

In the bustling markets of Morocco, ghriba, meaning "the mysterious," captivates with its unique blend of textures and exotic ingredients. These Moroccan shortbread cookies, rich with ground almonds and fragrant spices such as cinnamon and sesame seeds, boast a chewy interior and a crackly exterior. Ghriba is a testament to the rich culinary heritage of North Africa, where the influence of Arabic, Berber, and French traditions converges in a delightful array of flavors and textures. The

Mexican wedding cookie, or polvorón, speaks to the cultural fusion that characterizes Mexican baking. Rooted in Spanish culinary heritage, these crumbly delights are enriched with ground nuts, often pecans or walnuts, and generously dusted with powdered sugar. The buttery and nutty profile of polvorones makes them a popular treat during celebrations, including weddings, quinceañeras, and Christmas festivities. The tradition of sharing these cookies reflects the warmth and friendliness that define Mexican hospitality.

Exploring international cookie traditions not only introduces diverse flavors but also unveils the shared cultural significance of these delectable creations. Beyond their culinary appeal, cookies serve as vessels of tradition, encapsulating stories of migration, cultural exchange, and the passing down of recipes through generations. Each cookie, whether enjoyed in a bustling market, a family kitchen, or during festive gatherings, carries a community's collective memories and traditions, making it a delectable ambassador of cultural heritage.

Moreover, baking and sharing these international cookies fosters a sense of connection and understanding between people of different backgrounds. The exchange of recipes, techniques, and stories surrounding these cookies becomes a bridge that transcends language barriers and celebrates the universal joy derived from shared culinary experiences. It is a reminder that, despite our diverse cultural landscapes, savoring a cookie can unite us in a shared appreciation for these sweet treats' artistry and cultural significance.

In conclusion, exploring international cookie traditions is a delightful journey beyond taste, offering a glimpse into the rich cultural tapestry woven through baking and sharing. Each cookie becomes a passport to a different corner of the world, inviting us to savor the diverse flavors and the stories, traditions, and shared moments that make these treats unique. As we embark on this global culinary adventure, we discover that the language of cookies is universal, speaking to the shared joy, warmth, and connection that emanate from the simple act of breaking bread—or, in this case, sharing a cookie.

Recipes inspired by global flavors

Recipes inspired by global flavors weave a vibrant tapestry of culinary creativity, inviting us to embark on a journey that transcends geographical boundaries and explores the diverse richness of world cuisines. This culinary exploration goes beyond the familiar confines of our kitchens, transporting us to distant lands through the nuanced symphony of flavors, aromas, and textures that define each global culinary tradition. From India's aromatic spices to Japan's umami-laden delights, the world has become our pantry, and each ingredient carries a story, a history, and a unique sense of place.

In the heart of the Mediterranean, the flavors of Greece beckon with the freshness of olives, the brightness of lemons, and the richness of feta cheese. Inspired by the sun-drenched landscapes and the azure waters of the Aegean, Greek recipes bring forth a celebration of simplicity and wholesomeness. A classic like moussaka, with layers of eggplant, minced meat, and béchamel sauce, captures the essence of Greek comfort food, offering a taste of the country's culinary heritage. The bold flavors of oregano, garlic, and olive oil infuse souvlaki and tzatziki, creating a Mediterranean melody that resonates on the palate.

Journeying eastward to the vibrant streets of Thailand, the harmonious dance of sweet, sour, salty, and spicy flavors defines Thai cuisine. Tom Yum Goong, a fragrant and zesty shrimp soup, epitomizes the complexity and balance of Thai dishes. The interplay of lemongrass, galangal, kaffir lime leaves, and chili creates a sensory experience that reflects the country's tropical landscape. With its aromatic blend of herbs and coconut milk, Thai green curry offers a velvety and indulgent curry that is comforting and refreshing. These recipes invite us to explore Thailand's bold and dynamic flavors, where each bite is a journey through the bustling markets and vibrant street food stalls.

In the heartlands of Mexico, the soulful notes of corn, beans, and chilies come together to create a symphony of flavors that define the country's rich culinary tapestry. The humble taco, with its myriad fillings and salsas, represents the quintessence of Mexican street food. Whether filled with succulent carnitas, grilled fish, or spiced vegetables, the taco embodies the diversity and vibrancy of Mexican cuisine. The nuanced flavors of mole, a complex sauce made with a blend of chilies, spices, and chocolate, showcase the culinary artistry of Mexico, offering a rich and indulgent experience. Each bite tells a story of ancient civilizations, colonial influences, and the resilience of a culinary tradition that has stood the test of time.

Turning our gaze to the aromatic landscapes of India, a kaleidoscope of spices and herbs unfolds, creating a sensory journey that is both exhilarating and deeply satisfying. A dish like chicken tikka masala, with its succulent grilled chicken in a creamy and spiced tomato-based sauce, represents the fusion of Indian and British culinary influences. The fragrant biryani, with its layers of basmati rice, tender meat, and aromatic spices, encapsulates the grandeur and opulence of Indian feasts. The diversity of Indian cuisine, from the fiery curries of the south to the delicate flavors of northern cuisine, invites us to explore how spices can transform simple ingredients into a culinary masterpiece.

Heading south to the cultural crossroads of Africa, Moroccan cuisine's bold and earthy flavors captivate the senses. A tagine, with its slow-cooked blend of spices, fruits, and meats, offers a taste of the intricate culinary traditions of the Maghreb region. The fragrant couscous, paired with vegetables, dried fruits, and aromatic spices, represents the staple grain that has sustained North African communities for centuries. The art of preserving lemons, a common ingredient in Moroccan cooking, adds a tangy and citrusy note to dishes, showcasing the resourcefulness and ingenuity of the cuisine. Moroccan recipes, with their vibrant colors and bold flavors, reveal the influence of Berber, Arab, and French culinary traditions.

Across the vast expanse of China, a myriad of regional cuisines unfurls, each offering a unique perspective on the country's diverse culinary heritage. Sichuan cuisine, known for its fiery and numbing flavors, introduces dishes like map tofu, where tofu is bathed in a spicy and aromatic sauce. The delicate flavors of Cantonese cuisine shine in dim sum, with its array of steamed dumplings, buns, and savory treats. Influenced by the harsh winters, Northern Chinese cuisine features hearty dishes like Peking duck, showcasing the art of crispy skin and succulent meat. Chinese recipes, emphasizing balance, harmony, and seasonality, invite us to savor the nuances of a culinary tradition that spans millennia.

Japan, with its meticulous approach to ingredients and presentation, offers a culinary experience that is both refined and deeply rooted in tradition. Sushi, with its precise combination of vinegared rice, fresh fish, and seaweed, exemplifies the artistry and craftsmanship that define Japanese cuisine. Ramen, a beloved comfort food, boasts various flavors, from the rich and savory tonkatsu broth to the light and soy-based shoyu broth. The delicate flavors of matcha, whether enjoyed in traditional tea ceremonies or incorporated into desserts, showcase the reverence for nature and simplicity that permeate Japanese culinary philosophy. Japanese recipes, emphasizing seasonality and balance, reflect a culture that values the purity of flavors and the art of presentation.

The fusion of global flavors doesn't just stop at traditional recipes; it extends to the innovative and creative realm of fusion cuisine. In cosmopolitan hubs worldwide, chefs and home cooks draw inspiration from diverse culinary traditions, creating dishes that defy categorization and celebrate the beauty of cross-cultural influences. A sushi burrito, marrying the flavors of Japanese sushi with the convenience of a handheld burrito, represents the intersection of two distinct culinary worlds. Kimchi tacos, blending the spicy and fermented flavors of Korean kimchi with the familiar embrace of Mexican tortillas, showcase fusion cuisine's playful and inventive spirit. These recipes exemplify the dynamic and ever-evolving nature of global flavors, where culinary boundaries blur, and innovation becomes a celebration of diversity.

Exploring recipes inspired by global flavors is more than a culinary adventure; it is a celebration of cultural diversity, a recognition of shared human experiences, and a testament to the universal joy derived from breaking bread together. As we navigate the world through our kitchens, we not only savor the diverse and exquisite tastes that global recipes offer but also gain a deeper understanding of each dish's stories, traditions, and histories. It is a journey that transcends the limitations of language, connecting us to the heart and soul of different cultures through the universal language of food. In each recipe, whether drawn from the bustling markets of Marrakech, the serene tea fields of Japan, or the vibrant street food stalls of Mexico City, we discover not only the artistry of culinary traditions but also the shared humanity that binds us together in a tapestry of global flavors.

Connecting through the universal love of cookies

Connecting through the universal love of cookies transcends cultural, linguistic, and geographical boundaries, forging a delightful common ground where indulging in a sweet treat becomes a shared language of joy, comfort, and nostalgia. Cookies, those delectable morsels of baked goodness, have an uncanny ability to evoke cherished memories, create moments of togetherness, and bridge gaps between diverse individuals and communities. In the aromatic warmth of kitchens worldwide, the universal love for cookies becomes a thread that weaves through the fabric of human connection.

At the heart of this shared affection for cookies is the nostalgia they evoke—the comforting aroma wafting through the air, the anticipation of a first bite, and the flood of memories that transport individuals back to moments of childhood bliss. Whether it's the scent of freshly baked chocolate chip cookies, the warmth of gingerbread spices, or the buttery notes of shortbread, these aromas trigger a cascade of emotions that harken back to a time when life was simpler. The world seemed wrapped in the magic of homemade treats. The universal appeal of cookies lies not just in their flavors but in the ability to stir a collective sentimentality, reminding us of the warmth and love associated with baking and sharing.

With their infinite variety of shapes, textures, and flavors, cookies become a canvas for cultural expression, allowing communities worldwide to infuse their unique identity into these delectable creations. Whether it's the crumbly elegance of French madeleines, the spice-laden intrigue of Moroccan riba, or the gooey richness of American brownies, each cookie tells a story of cultural heritage, regional ingredients, and the nuanced artistry passed down through generations. In this way, cookies become more than just a sugary delight—they become edible tales of tradition, offering a taste of the world's diverse culinary landscapes.

Moreover, baking and sharing cookies becomes a universal language that fosters connections within families, friends, and communities. From grandmothers passing down secret recipes to grandchildren to friends gathering for an afternoon of cookie exchange, the shared baking experience creates bonds beyond the kitchen. Passing along a cookie recipe isn't just about transferring ingredients and instructions; it's a transference of love, heritage, and a piece of one's culinary identity. It's a connection that spans generations, carrying with it the essence of shared laughter, stories, and wisdom embedded in the tradition of baking.

The universality of cookies is most evident during festive seasons when these sweet treats become ambassadors of celebration, symbolizing joy, abundance, and the spirit of giving. Whether it's Christmas sugar cookies adorned with colorful icing, Hanukkah rugelach filled with sweet fruit and nuts, or Diwali's aromatic ghee-laden sweets, cookies are central to the world's diverse celebrations. Gifting cookies during festive occasions transcends cultural and religious divides, embodying a shared understanding that the sweetness of life is best celebrated when shared with others.

In an era where technology connects us across vast distances, the love of cookies finds a contemporary expression in online communities, where enthusiasts share recipes, exchange baking tips, and showcase their cookie creations. Social media platforms, blogs, and virtual cookie exchanges become digital spaces where individuals from different corners unite under a shared passion for baking. The universal language of cookies, spoken through captivating images and engaging narratives, creates a virtual community that transcends borders, fostering friendships among people who may never meet face-to-face but are connected through the shared love of this humble yet beloved baked delight.

The universality of cookies extends beyond the kitchen and the screen to become a powerful vehicle for philanthropy and social impact. Whether organized by local communities or global corporations, Cookie sales often serve as fundraisers for charitable causes. Events like bake sales for disaster relief, cookie drives for community development, or campaigns for medical research funding leverage the widespread appeal of cookies to mobilize resources and unite people to support common goals. The simple pleasure derived from a cookie purchase becomes a catalyst for positive change, turning the act of indulgence into a force for good.

The emotional resonance of cookies is evident in "cookie culture," where cookies are not just baked goods but cultural symbols that represent shared experiences and sentiments. The rise of cookie influencers, dedicated Instagram accounts, and viral cookie challenges reflect a global fascination with the artistry of cookie creation. The act of decorating cookies, experimenting with flavors, and pushing the boundaries of traditional recipes becomes a form of creative expression that resonates with a diverse and engaged audience. In this way, cookies transcend their humble origins to become cultural artifacts that speak to the shared human experience of finding joy, creativity, and connection in life's simple pleasures.

Connecting through the universal love of cookies isn't solely about the act of baking and consuming these delightful treats; it's about embracing the values they represent. Cookies embody the principles of generosity, sharing, and the universal pursuit of happiness. The simplicity of a cookie belies its profound ability to evoke feelings of warmth, comfort, and community. Whether enjoyed with a cup of tea in London, as part of a traditional tea ceremony in Japan, or dunked into milk on a suburban American kitchen table, cookies create a sense of kinship that transcends cultural differences and unites us in our shared humanity.

In conclusion, the universal love of cookies is a testament to the power of food to unite people. With their diverse flavors, textures, and cultural significance, cookies become a conduit for shared joy, memories, and the celebration of life's simple pleasures. Baking and sharing cookies become a universal language that speaks to our longing for connection, understanding, and the shared experience of savoring life's sweet moments. In this global celebration of cookies, we discover the richness of culinary diversity and the common thread of human connection that binds us all in the delightful embrace of a timeless and universally loved treat.

CONCLUSION

In the delightful journey through the pages of "Journey into Classic Crinkles and Sugar Sparkles: Timeless Favorites," we have explored the rich tapestry of classic cookie recipes, cultural significances, iconic moments in cookie history, and the artistry involved in creating these delectable treats. From the origins and evolution of traditional cookie recipes to the exploration of international cookie traditions, this e-book has celebrated the universal love for cookies.

As we immersed ourselves in classic crinkles and sugar sparkles, we uncovered the stories behind each recipe, the cultural significance embedded in every bite, and the emotional connections that cookies foster across generations. We delved into the intricacies of baking, from essential tools and ingredients to tips for perfecting the art of cookie-making, addressing common challenges, and exploring variations that add a creative twist to these timeless favorites.

The e-book has guided novice and seasoned bakers, offering step-by-step instructions for making perfect crinkles, exploring the world of sugar sparkles and their variations, and providing insights into unique ingredients and flavor combinations. We navigated through the emotional connection to classic cookies, discovering the stories and memories associated with these treats, and explored ways to create new memories with classic crinkles and sugar sparkles.

From adapting classic recipes for dietary preferences to tips for successful gluten-free and vegan baking, the e-book addressed the evolving landscape of culinary preferences, ensuring that all can experience the joy of classic cookies. We also delved into gifting, hosting cookie exchange parties, and spreading love through homemade treats, showcasing how these delightful creations can be shared and enjoyed in myriad ways.

In the final chapters, we embraced innovation while preserving tradition explored trendy ingredients and techniques for a contemporary twist, and encouraged readers to develop their unique crinkle or sparkle recipes. We provided tips for experimenting with flavors and textures, sharing creations with friends and family, and even venturing into fusion recipes that combine classic and modern tastes.

In essence, "Journey into Classic Crinkles and Sugar Sparkles" has been more than a collection of recipes; it has celebrated the universal love for cookies. Whether you're a seasoned baker looking to perfect your craft or someone embarking on the exciting journey of cookie-making for the first time, this e-book has served as a guide, a source of inspiration, and a reminder that, in the simple act of baking and sharing cookies, we find joy, connection, and the timeless magic of a treat that transcends cultural and culinary boundaries. May your kitchen be filled with the aroma of freshly baked crinkles and sugar sparkles, and may each bite carry with it the warmth and camaraderie that these timeless favorites bring to our lives. Happy baking!

Thank you for buying and reading/ listening to our book. If you found this book useful/ helpful please take a few minutes and leave a review on the platform where you purchased our book. Your feedback matters greatly to us.

9 798869 123145